Judge Not

Judge Not

ANDRÉ GIDE

Translated from the French
and with an Introduction and Notes
by Benjamin Ivry

University of Illinois Press
Urbana and Chicago

Ne jugez pas © 1969 by Éditions Gallimard
English translation © 2003 by the Board of Trustees
of the University of Illinois
C 5 4 3 2 1

⊗ This book is printed on acid-free paper.

Library of Congress Cataloging-in-Publication Data
Gide, André, 1869–1951.
[Ne jugez pas. English]
Judge not / André Gide ; translated from the French
and with an introduction by Benjamin Ivry.
p.   cm.
Includes bibliographical references.
ISBN 0-252-02844-9 (cloth : alk. paper)
1. Crime—France. 2. Criminals—France. 3. Justice,
Administration of—France. I. Ivry, Benjamin.
II. Gide, André, 1869–1951. Souvenirs de la Cour d'assises. English.
III. Gide, André, 1869–1951. Affaire Redureau. English.
IV. Gide, André, 1869–1951. Séquestrée de Poitiers. English.
V. Title.
HV6963.N5313   2003
364.944—dc21   2002152245

Contents

Introduction:
Bearing Witness

Benjamin Ivry

André Gide's striking qualities as a man and writer included his will-ingness to bear responsibility, to say what he felt had to be said and do what had to be done. Gide (1869–1951) was admirably courageous and free-spirited, possessed with a driving curiosity about literature, natural history, and human behavior. As one devotee said, Gide was a "great learner."[1] In writing *Ne jugez pas* (*Judge Not*), his goals included learn-ing about the judicial system, news items, and the motivations of crimi-nals. When he produced most of the material collected in *Ne jugez pas,* Gide was almost sixty years old. He had already published the novels that would make his lasting reputation, including *Les Caves du Vatican* (*The Vatican Swindle;* 1914) and *Les Faux-monnayeurs* (*The Counter-feiters;* 1926). He had written a celebrated two-part journal of an Afri-can trip in which he protested colonial exploitation, *Voyage au Congo* (*Travels in the Congo;* 1927) and *Le Retour du Tchad* (*Return from Lake Chad;* 1928). He had also published extended essays on writers such as Joseph Conrad and Emile Verhaeren (both 1927) and his *Essai sur Montaigne* (1929). His polemic text defending pederasty, *Corydon* (1924), had won him enemies, as had the frank account of gay experi-ences in his autobiographical work *Si le grain ne meurt* (*If It Die . . . ;*) (1926). Acutely aware of social prejudices and inequities, he focused his attention on courtroom subjects and news items with his usual seri-ousness and sobriety.

1. Walter Benjamin, *Selected Writings,* 2 vols. (1927-34), ed. Rodney Livingstone et al., trans. Michael W. Jennings, Howard Eiland, and Gary Smith (Cambridge, Mass.: Harvard Univer-sity Press, 1999), 2:95.

Ne jugez pas gathers into one volume the following writings: *Souvenirs de la cour d'assises* (A memoir of the assize court; 1914); *L'Affaire Redureau* (The Redureau case; 1930); *Faits divers* (News items; 1926–27); and *La Séquestrée de Poitiers* (The confined woman of Poitiers; 1930). Some writers have seen the texts in *Ne jugez pas* as predominantly social rather than personal. Gide took judicial matters quite personally, however, using courtroom experiences to illuminate his own fiction and life. His novels and essays often involve legal matters and abnormal or antisocial behavior. When the writer Walter Benjamin told Gide that he was called "the poet of the exceptional case," Gide replied: "That's certainly true. But why should that be? Day after day, we encounter modes of behavior and people who by their very existence invalidate our existing norms. A large share of our ordinary everyday decisions, as well as our extraordinary ones, are not susceptible to judgment by traditional moral values. Because this is so, it is necessary to focus on such cases, to scrutinize them, without cowardice or cynicism."[2]

Generations of readers saw Gide's novels as refreshingly antitraditional, breaking free from the doctrines of writers such as Maurice Barrès, who urged that Frenchmen should feel "rooted" (*enraciné*) in their land. Gide studied people who chose to be rootless by undermining conventions, considering them to be essential models for any creative life. The motivations behind this attitude were many. For one thing, Gide believed his own Protestant heritage to contain a passion for truth.[3]

Gide was also fascinated by abnormal and criminal behavior because he had published partial accounts and defenses of his own sex life as a pederast at a time when homosexuality was illegal and severely punished, as happened in the notorious case of his friend Oscar Wilde. Every time he pursued the real object of his desires, Gide committed a crime, although his personal fortune, social status, and fame as a writer protected him in the France of that day.

In their depictions of transgressors, Gide's novels and essays con-

2. Ibid., 2:96.
3. André Gide, *Journals,* 4 vols., trans. Justin O'Brien, with an introduction by Richard Howard (Urbana: University of Illinois Press, 2000), 2:339.

tinue the tradition of writers such as Dostoyevsky and Conrad, many of whose books also focus on criminal protagonists, as a basis for better understanding human motivations and society. In *Ne jugez pas* Gide examined—among other subjects—his attitude to jury service, the way the young murderer Redureau is prosecuted, and a crime that underlined the horrors of provincial life in Poitiers. These texts have received comparatively little sustained attention and for the most part have never before been published in English.[4] The translator of Gide's journals, Justin O'Brien, dismissed them as "collections of gory documents," adding: "In the course of pursuing this morbid hobby, Gide *seemed* to be preaching the fullest expression of the least honorable instincts."[5]

More than a "morbid hobby," Gide's investigations relate to essential parts of his life and creativity, as I will show. Gide's biographer Alan Sheridan states that news items provided the writer with "narrative elements that were not autobiographical: they represented an escape from self and from the history of that self."[6] Nevertheless, *L'Affaire Redureau* and *La Sequestrée de Poitiers* reflect a certain personalization, perhaps due in part to Gide's habit of dictating texts to a typist. As the 1930s progressed, Gide's personal involvement in social matters would develop even more as he abandoned fiction writing, culminating with a temporary fascination with Communism and an eye-opening trip to the Soviet Union, recounted in *Retour de l'U.R.S.S* (*Back from the USSR;* 1936).

A Memoir of the Assize Court

The earliest text presented here is the product of a term of jury duty in 1912. Unlike many people, Gide actively sought to serve on a jury and made several requests over a period of years before he was finally appointed. He served in Rouen, where his family's home was located. At the time the French press and public were in an uproar over many is-

---

4. *Souvenirs de la cour d'assises* appeared in a now long-unavailable British edition: André Gide, *Recollections of the Assize Court,* trans. Philip A. Wilkins (London: Hutchinson, 1941).
5. Justin O'Brien, *Portrait of Andre Gide: A Critical Biography* (New York: Knopf, 1953), 191.
6. Alan Sheridan, *André Gide: A Life in the Present* (London: Hamish Hamilton, 1998), 269.

sues involving the jury system, such as the method of selecting jurors, procedures for questioning witnesses, the completeness of information given to a jury, and the appointment rather than election of jury foremen. Gide expressed himself on these subjects in the newspaper *L'Opinion* in 1913.[7] His experience as a juror taught him above all else that human justice is "doubtful and precarious." As a writer Gide brought special qualities to his analysis of such matters. Since the accused usually belonged to a social class different from that of the judges, the two could often not even understand each other in the courtroom. Gide made a special effort to think through defendants' arguments, but he observed that judges and the other jurors usually did not.

In the case of an arsonist, Gide mused that the accused might have set fires for a "sexual thrill" (*jouissance sexuelle*), but the judges, apparently unaware of this possible explanation, decided that the crime was inexplicable. Long before his jury experience, Gide was convinced of the value of the injunction "Judge not," from Christ's Sermon on the Mount. In November 1896 he wrote to a friend that Parisians were overly prone to criticism, adding: "The beginning of wisdom is in this expression from the Gospel: 'Judge not.'"[8] Watching the wheels of justice turn was a highly emotional experience for Gide; eighteen years after the sessions, he still vividly recalled "the atrocious anguish that used to take hold of [him] at the Rouen Assize Court."[9] These emotions added drama and urgency to his memoir. Gide notes with barely concealed outrage how the accused were judged according to their appearance and social class. He felt that judgment was God's duty, not man's, and human justice in its essence must be flawed.

Jury duty provided Gide equal measures of exhilaration and exhaustion. He wrote to his friend the stage director Jacques Copeau during

7. André Gide, *The Correspondence of Andre Gide and Edmund Gosse, 1904-1928*, ed. and with a translation, introduction, and notes by Linette F. Brugmans (New York: New York University Press, 1959), 111.

8. André Gide, *Correspondance, 1895-1950, Andre Gide-Andre Ruyters*, ed. Claude Martin and Victor Martin-Schmets, with the collaboration, for the introduction, of Pierre Masson, 2 vols. (Lyon: Presses Universitaires de Lyon, 1990), 1:16. (All translations from French are my own.) In the letter to Ruyters, Gide uses the more emphatic form of the command, *Ne jugez point* (Thou shalt not judge), instead of *Ne jugez pas* (Judge not).

9. Gide, *Journals*, 3:135.

the sessions: "It's as exhausting as crossing a *chott* [an Algerian salt lake]. More than ever, I wished that you were by my side. During the first session yesterday . . . Ah, if only you'd been there. How you would have benefited. I took four pages of notes and eight this morning, from memory. Amazing."[10]

The theatrical aspects of the hearings were of potential interest to Copeau, he suggests. Nine days later he wrote to Copeau: "My pen is quite clumsy[;] you understand that I'm exhausted. . . . I am having ideas of all colors, but mainly ultraviolet and infrared."[11] Gide perceived the human reality behind the drama of courtroom confrontations and went out of his way to help the prisoner Henri Lebrun, whose name would be changed to Yves Cordier in *Souvenirs*. Lebrun had fallen in with a group of thieves out of weakness of character rather than iniquity, and Gide's efforts to get the prisoner's sentence commuted are only partly recounted in *Souvenirs*. Four years later he was still trying to help Lebrun. He appealed to the writer Valéry Larbaud, informing him that after his jail sentence, Lebrun had joined the army and been wounded. Lebrun was hospitalized in Vichy, where Larbaud lived, and Gide told his friend about the matter:

> [The wounded man] has no one on earth but myself to look out for him. He's the poor young shoemaker who got trapped in a stupid case I had to decide when I was a juror. He's a very fine boy who was the victim of an abominable denial of justice, after which I was able to intervene in a manner to lessen his sentence. He was finally going to return to life when the war broke out—I tell his story in detail in my *Souvenirs de la cour d'assises* (while changing the names). . . . I'm sure this boy will interest you greatly. Especially as I sense that he has the greatest need for affection, and any foolishness he did was always done "to help other people."[12]

10. André Gide, *Correspondance André Gide-Jacques Copeau,* ed. Jean Claude, introduction by Claude Sicard, Cahiers André Gide, vols. 12-13 (Paris: Gallimard, 1987-88), 1:39 (entry for May 14, 1912). In his journal entry for November 15, 1930, Gide recalled the sense of "horrible anguish that used to grip" him at the Rouen assize court (*Journals*, 3:135; my revision of O'Brien's translation).

11. Gide, *Correspondance Gide-Copeau,* 42 (letter dated May 23, 1912).

12. André Gide, *Correspondance André Gide, Valery Larbaud: 1905-1938,* ed. and with an introduction by Françoise Lioure (Paris: Gallimard, 1989), 171-72 (letter dated May 19, 1916).

The emotions felt during jury duty remained acute for years. In 1926, when Gide's friend the novelist Jean Schlumberger stated that he was about to begin jury duty, Gide excitedly exclaimed: "Congratulations, it may disturb your work, but it's worth it. You know, it takes a long time to get over, as if you had suffered a bout of typhoid! I myself needed a convalescence afterward, as I was in such a state of nervous tension and emotion! Above all, take notes, old man, take notes and try to ask questions from the first session onward, otherwise you'll never dare to try again."[13]

Indeed, Gide worked on his notes for *Souvenirs* while taking a cure in the sulfur baths at Tivoli, Italy, to soothe his nerves. (For contrast and variety, he worked at the same time on a French translation of poems written in English by the Bengali writer Rabindranath Tagore.) *Souvenirs* was reworked from Gide's initial notes not just by changing names but by emphasizing certain experiences and omitting others and sometimes shifting the order of events. It is a crafted work, although it can appear to be a mere transcription. Gide would later judge *Souvenirs* harshly as prose, stating that it had "no more to do with literature" than did *Voyage au Congo* or *Le Retour de l'U.R.S.S.*[14] Nevertheless, it is of primary importance for understanding Gide as a social critic and activist. As do a number of his nonfiction works, it shows him saying something because it needed to be said.

This motive puzzled some of his upper-crust society friends. The British professor of literature Edmund Gosse saw it as a "divagation" from Gide's "customary path," as he told Gide in a letter: "My first exclamation (when I saw the first installment in the *Nouvelle revue*) was 'What can he have to say about juries and judges and prisoners at the bar?' But I had only to read a couple of pages to see that your profound sincerity, applied to this hackneyed and vulgarised subject, drew it

13. M. Saint-Clair, *Les Cahiers de la Petite Dame; notes pour l'histoire authentique d'André Gide*, 4 vols., Cahiers André Gide, vol. 4 (Paris: Gallimard, 1973-77), 1:350.

14. Gide, *Journals*, 4:288 (my revision of O'Brien's translation). For a comprehensive presentation of notes and variants, see André Gide, *Souvenirs et voyages*, ed. Pierre Masson, with the collaboration of Daniel Durosay and Martine Sagaert (Paris: Gallimard/Bibliothèque de la Pléiade, 2001), 1083-90.

straight up out of the commonplace and gave it style."[15] Perhaps not realizing that *Souvenirs* was no mere exercise in style for Gide, Gosse added, "I read right through the book . . . and was hungry for more at the end. But you must not indulge this hunger. You have other and larger fish to fry."[16]

Gide would not have agreed that there are subjects "larger" than the contrast between human and divine justice. The society painter Jacques-Émile Blanche was equally baffled, writing to Gide in October 1916, "Do you know we tried to read them several times with . . . difficulty, the Rouen notes? They are uninteresting, and I don't understand why! At any rate, the fact that they are uninteresting is their major interest!"[17]

Nevertheless, the book did find sympathetic and vocal readers, such as Klaus Mann, the son of the novelist Thomas Mann, who in 1943 called *Souvenirs* an "entertaining and instructive little book."[18] Mann noted that for Gide "to come out for the underprivileged, against the rulers and judges, foreshadows or already implies a truly revolutionary spirit. Books like *Corydon* and *Les Souvenirs de la cour d'assize* [sic] contradict and arraign certain principles and practices of the bourgeois order. The fight for certain minorities results almost inevitably in social criticism."[19]

The Redureau Case

In his review of *L'Affaire Redureau,* the French philosopher Gabriel Marcel stated that Gide could be considered "as an entomologist."[20]

15. Gide, *Correspondence of Gide and Gosse, 1904-1928,* 110 (letter dated April 6, 1914).
16. Ibid.
17. André Gide, *Correspondance André Gide-Jacques-Émile Blanche, 1892-1939,* ed. Georges-Paul Collet (Paris: Gallimard, 1979), 195-96. Social consciousness transcended the question of personal sexuality. Edmund Gosse, a discreet upper-class British homosexual, was not interested in class struggles, whereas Klaus Mann, a gay writer from a younger generation, was.
18. Klaus Mann, *Gide and the Crisis of Modern Thought* (New York: Creative Age, 1943), 120.
19. Ibid.
20. Gabriel Marcel, "L'Affaire Redureau et La Séquestrée de Poitiers," *La Quinzaine critique,* no. 25 (January 17, 1931).

Gide was in fact an enthusiastic amateur entomologist and naturalist. According to a friend, when he first saw his infant daughter Catherine in 1924, he examined her "as an entomologist would."[21] With this patient eye for detail, Gide studied the case of a fifteen-year old vineyard laborer, Marcel Redureau, who inexplicably butchered his employer's family. As Gide explains in his introduction, part of the mystery is understanding why a gentle and obedient boy suddenly committed savage murders with no apparent warning. Nothing in the boy's previous actions or appearance predicted the tragedy.

As he fully documents in his journals and correspondence, Gide was continually on the prowl for fifteen-year-old boys—his ideal sexual partners—in cinemas, trains, and the countryside. His biographers have noted, not quite correctly, that Gide "never got caught" as a result of his pederastic proclivities.[22] When he found a potential sexual partner, detailed observation and a deft approach were essential to avoid any adverse reaction. He told Maria van Rysselberghe in 1922 about his constant hunt: "What I find so attractive is a sort of sensual gluttony, almost an appeal, that I sense in some boys. That's why I've rarely made a mistake and, so far, avoided scandal."[23]

Marcel Redureau's crime could not have been predicted by observing his appearance or behavior, which must have particularly fascinated a writer who frequently made instant evaluations of unknown fifteen-year-old boys as part of patient, skilled, and studied seductions. Gide acknowledged that his sexual tastes led him "toward pleasure, frenzy, risk, the unknown."[24]

21. Roger Martin du Gard, *Journal*, 3 vols., ed. Claude Sicard (Paris: Gallimard, 1992-93), 2:413.

22. Saint-Clair, *Cahiers*, 1:13-14. In 1918 Gide told Maria Van Rysselberghe about his having "misbehaved" with a young boy in Grantchester, England, where his lover, Marc Allégret, was boarding with a British family. Gide said he did so "without desire or curiosity, as a matter of form." The boy told his mother, who informed Marc's teacher, who warned Marc in turn. Marc defended his "uncle's" kind influence and told Gide with a smile, "All the same, Uncle André, try to avoid any more 'matters of form.'"

23. Ibid., 151. Van Rysselberghe noted that Gide's sexuality, "'while so profound, so demanding, so irresistible,' could be satisfied 'so easily, so lightly, and turn so quickly into exaltation'" (quoted in Sheridan, *Gide*, 437).

24. Saint-Clair, *Cahiers*, 1:717. If a boy was clearly willing, Gide would request mutual masturbation, "face to face." See Martin du Gard, *Journal*, 2:232-33. Gide's sexual expectations are summarized in Sheridan, *Gide*, 344-45.

Moreover, Gide had also cast himself emotionally in the role of murder victim, metaphorically if not actually. In 1918 his wife, Madeleine, had burned all his letters to her—more than thirty years of deeply personal writing—after he departed on a trip to England with his new adolescent lover, Marc Allégret. When he learned that the letters were gone, the usually restrained Gide stated: "I thought I was dying. . . . Ah, I can imagine what a father might feel on arriving home and being told by his wife, 'Our child is dead. I have killed him.'"[25] The following year Gide told Maria Van Rysselberghe: "I avoided madness and suicide. . . . I still cannot face the disappearance of those letters."[26] In 1924, during a bout of appendicitis, Gide told Martin du Gard: "You see, I died a few years ago, when I discovered that my wife had burned all my letters to better disconnect from me, to cross me out of her life."[27] Feeling like a murder victim, even metaphorically, may have led Gide to focus more intently on murderers' motivations.

But Gide did not merely empathize with crime victims, as he explained on other occasions. Around 1896 Gide made the following entry to his journal, under the heading "Literature and Ethics": "'There are no crimes, however great, that on certain days I have not felt capable of committing,' Goethe said. The greatest minds are also the most capable of great crimes, which they generally do not commit, because of wisdom, because of love, or because they would limit themselves by so doing."[28] Gide's journals express a number of extreme emotional states, which may have brought him closer to understanding a criminal's thought processes: "Yesterday, abominable relapse, which leaves my body and mind in a state bordering on despair, suicide, madness."[29]

The lasting incomprehensibility of Redureau's crime made it a particularly stimulating subject for Gide's reflections on the permanent mystery of human interactions.

---

25. Sheridan, *Gide,* 314.
26. Saint-Clair, *Cahiers,* 1:10 (entry for January 10, 1919).
27. Roger Martin du Gard, *Notes sur André Gide, 1913-1951* (Paris: Gallimard, 1951), 83.
28. Gide, *Journals,* 1:71.
29. Ibid., 2:156 (entry dated October 15, 1916).

News Items

Gide began to collect news clippings at age twenty-one, at the same time he decided to become a writer.[30] Years later his daughter, Catherine, located three dozen folders containing around six hundred press cuttings, dating from 1891 onward. The folders have titles such as Boxing Matches, Confinements (Séquéstrations), Pederasty, Swindles and Embezzlements, Shipwrecks/Tragedies at Sea, Disasters and Catastrophes, and Morality Cases. Some of Gide's fictional works were directly inspired by such news items, among them *Isabelle, Les Caves du Vatican,* and *Les Faux-monnayeurs.* In articles in the *Nouvelle revue française,* Gide requested that readers send him their own clippings, thereby proposing a kind of collaboration with the reading public. Instead of developing news items into fiction, *Faits divers* presents the news items themselves, noting how easily journalistic language falls into clichés instead of making a serious attempt to express the reality of events.

An item about the suicide of a high-school student inspired Gide to develop a story line in his novel *Les Faux-monnayeurs.* In a series of cuttings he further documented suicides by social outcasts. Many of these stories involve Russians, no doubt partly because Gide was fascinated with, as the writer Boris de Schloezer called it, Dostoyevsky's "war against morality," which was "religious in essence."[31] Roger Martin du Gard believed that Gide published his daring defense of pederasty, *Corydon,* only because he was suffering from "Slavic intoxication" after preparing public lectures on Dostoyevsky for Copeau's theater. Martin du Gard, along with most of Gide's friends, considered the publication of *Corydon* to be like a "nostalgic call to martyrdom," adding: "Like the hero of a Russian novel, [Gide] burns to defy society and offer himself up to be pummeled. He aspires to outrage, to receive opprobrium and the pillory."[32] For Gide, Russian murderers and religious fanatics attained the vehemence that he treasured, which Walter Benjamin called a "principled rejection of every golden mean, a com-

30. Elizabeth R. Jackson, "André Gide et les faits-divers: un rapport preliminaire," *Bulletin des amis d'André Gide* 20, no. 93 (January 1992): 83–91.

31. Cited in Martin du Gard, *Notes,* 51.

32. Ibid., 46.

mitment to extremes."[33] The news items were offered as a mirror of Gide's own inner concerns. Some are absurd, mixing grotesque comedy with misery, while others recount stark tragedies.

Gide's curiosity and fascination conquered almost everything, even when he was present at a tragic event. In 1916 Gide and Madeleine were involved in a train crash in which several passengers were killed and many injured. He observed: "Again I note my great difficulty in taking tragically, even seriously, a random accident. I remain amused, as at a show, or excited, and ready to put forth a great reserve of sudden activity."[34]

Sharing his excitement at discovery, Gide dedicated certain news clippings to friends. An account of the Jack Johnson–Jim Jeffries boxing match in Reno, Nevada, in 1910 is dedicated to the author Jean Prévost, a boxing fan. For another clipping, Gide borrowed the title "The Child Who Accuses Himself" from an article published by his friend Jean Schlumberger in the November 1919 issue of the *Nouvelle revue française*: "L'Enfant qui s'accuse: Contribution à l'étude de la criminalité enfantine." In 1911 Schlumberger had told Gide about a young farmhand who admitted stealing a purse but was later found to be innocent of the crime. Gide replied in a letter: "As for the story of the little thief, it's absolutely stunning. If one day I might recount the almost imperceptible transition from play to crime, that would be my finest book."[35] Gide's character Lafcadio in *Les Faux-monnayeurs* may illustrate this transition, in what many indeed consider to be Gide's best achievement in fiction.

Clippings were also a source of information about gay life at a time when few serious books were available about the subject. In extensive discussions and correspondence with gay friends including Martin du Gard, Jef Last, Jean Schlumberger, Henri Ghéon, and others, Gide was characteristically inquisitive. News items were avidly discussed, such as a 1903 scandal in which Parisian telegraph boys were revealed as prostitutes.[36]

---

33. Benjamin, *Selected Writings*, 2:95.

34. Gide, *Journals*, 2:131 (entry dated March 2, 1916).

35. André Gide, *Correspondance 1901–1950, André Gide–Jean Schlumberger*, ed. Pascal Mercier and Peter Fawcett (Paris: Gallimard, 1993), 389 (letter dated June 6, 1911).

36. Henri Ghéon, *Correspondance [de] Henri Ghéon [et] André Gide*, ed. Jean Tipy, introduction and notes by Anne-Marie Moulènes and Jean Tipy (Paris: Gallimard, 1976), 694–95.

The Confined Woman of Poitiers

La Séquestrée de Poitiers was a splashy news subject at the turn of the century. For Gide, the tale of the respected Monnier family's imprisoning Blanche exposed the squalid cruelties of provincial life. He would be haunted by Blanche Monnier's fate, mentioning her in letters and journals decades later. Gide was most likely aware of the trial when it occurred in 1901. In 1929 he reexamined documents that had been gathered by his old friend Charles Chanvin, a poet and lawyer. Chanvin was assisted by Jean-Paul Allégret, the brother of Gide's lover Marc Allégret. Jean-Paul would die of tuberculosis the following year, at age thirty-six. The book's uncredited editor, Louis Martin-Chauffier, arranged the documents for Gide, who then dictated his own presentation of the case. Gide found that Martin-Chauffier's version was often faulty, and he was obliged to look up the original texts as gathered by Chanvin and Allégret.[37]

In August 1929 Gide's friend Maria Van Rysselberghe saw him open a carton full of red and pink papers and take out some typed-up newspaper articles. They were from "the old days, the objective period of which he was speaking." Van Rysselberghe continued: "It was full of amusing things. How could I have forgotten the whole story of the confined woman of Poitiers, which once again is being brought up for consideration?" Looking at the folder put together by Chanvin, Gide said, "'This might have tempted me to do something, but I already have too many projects in hand." Then he opened the file, Van Rysselberghe recalled, looked for the most telling passages, "and got caught up in it once more."[38] Two months later Gide again brought the *Séquestrée* material to Van Rysselberghe, who did not share his enthusiasm: "[It]

37. Martin-Chauffier would also serve as editor for a never-completed collection of Gide's works: *Oeuvres complètes* (Gallimard, 1932–39). For details on Gide's composition of *La Séquestrée de Poitiers*, see Gide, *Journals*, 3:64 (entry for September 29, 1929) and 3:69 (entry for October 11, 1929). For information on Blanche Monnier, see Jean-Marie Augustin, *L'Histoire véridique de la Séquestrée de Poitiers* (Paris: Fayard, 2001). For the legal aspects of the case, see Jean Pradel and André Varinard, *Les Grands Arrêts du droit criminel*, 2 vols., 3d ed. (Paris: Sirey, 1992), 2:309–16.

38. Saint-Clair, *Cahiers*, 2:39–40. Van Rysselberghe added, "I never felt more with what avidity and gluttony he could be gripped by what is odd, or strange, which always seems to him more revelatory; it's as if it suddenly enlarged the human condition for him. I've only known [the Belgian poet Emile] Verhaeren to have an equal appetite" (Cahiers André Gide, vol. 5, 40).

still seemed more monstrous than odd to me, and more odd than interesting. I told him so. 'And you don't see it in the *N.R.F.*?' 'Not at all.'"[39]

Indeed, the story was not submitted to the august *Nouvelle revue française,* instead appearing as an independent pamphlet in 1930. Five years later Gide informed Van Rysselberghe that the French nightclub singer Marianne Oswald had approached him with her "dream" of portraying the title character onscreen. The year before, in 1934, Yves Allégret, Marc's socially conscious brother, had suggested that the subject might make a film. At first Gide had "shrugged" at this suggestion, but later he decided that it was a "highly treatable" subject from which might be drawn "some surprising effects on the subject of the atmosphere of provincial life." Van Rysselberghe was "choked" with objections, arguing that the subject was not suited for film, but Gide retorted that the actors involved would be excellent, and it was an opportunity to "indict society, which would widen the movie's scope."[40]

To further advance the project, Gide noted extensive "psychological instructions" for an unnamed future screenwriter.[41] A director was chosen, the great French filmmaker Jean Renoir (1894–1979), who would shortly thereafter create two masterpieces, *La Grande Illusion* (1937) and *La Règle du jeu* (1939). In January 1936 Gide took Van Rysselberghe to the film studio at Boulogne-Billancourt, just outside Paris, for a screening of Renoir's film *Toni* (1934), also attended by Marianne Oswald. The film made an "excellent impression," as did *La Grande Illusion,* which Gide saw later and admired for its "moral bearing at a time when there are so many foreigners in Paris."[42]

39. Saint-Clair, *Cahiers,* 2:53.

40. Ibid., 501; Marianne Oswald (1901–85), born Marianne Colin, of French origin in German territory, enjoyed a successful early career as a singer in Berlin. After the rise of fascism in 1933, she fled to Paris, where she performed at the well-known cabaret Le Boeuf sur le Toit. She spent World War II in America. Oswald was friendly with writers such as Jean Cocteau, Albert Camus, and Jacques Prévert, as well as Gide. A selection of her recordings has appeared on a compact disc, *L'Art de Marianne Oswald 1932 à 1937* (EPM Musique 982272 ADE660, 1992). Her memoir, *One Small Voice* (New York: McGraw-Hill, 1945), was published first in English and later in French as *Je n'ai pas appris à vivre* (I never learned how to live) (Paris: Domat, 1948).

41. Saint-Clair, *Cahiers,* 2:509 (entry for January 3, 1936). These notes have not been located.

42. Ibid., 3:25. Although Marc Allégret (1900–1973) and his brother Yves (1907–87) were film directors, they both ceded to Renoir as possible director of *La Séquestrée.* Marc usually made unpretentious comedies that relied on star power; Yves was more interested in social problems, but he was considered an uneven director. For more on Marc and Yves Allégret, see Bernard J. Houssiau, *Marc Allégret: découvreur de stars: sous les yeux d'André Gide* (Yens/Morges: Cabédita, 1994).

The *Séquestrée* film was never made, a tantalizing missed opportunity. The book received wide publicity, however, even without the added boost of a screen version. When its publication was announced in the press, his friend the novelist Jean-Richard Bloch (1884–1947), then living in Poitiers, invited him to visit the "sad and secretive city," even though he doubted that Gide's book would be "a realistic study, or contain more than a small bit of local color."[43] Bloch was probably surprised to find that Gide's work was in fact composed of press cuttings, full of local color.

When the book appeared, not all Gide's friends shared Van Rysselberghe's distaste for the subject. Thea Sternheim, wife of the German author Carl Sternheim, made it a kind of running gag in letters to Gide, writing to him that she was burdened with family responsibilities but adding, "Nothing is more contrary to my nature than to play this kind of *Séquestrée de Poitiers* role." When Gide sent her a copy of his *Journal* in 1939, Sternheim apologized for not writing sooner, saying she had been "sequestered from all [her] strength" by a cold when his gift "appeared one fine day in [her] good back-Malampia," echoing one of Blanche Monnier's favorite incomprehensible phrases.[44]

Gide himself kept *La Séquestrée* in mind over a number of years. George Painter points out that in his novel *La Symphonie pastorale* (1919) the protagonist Gertrude is discovered in a state of "verminous filth and apparent idiocy" that corresponds with the story of Blanche Monnier, whom her brother called by the pet name of Gertrude.[45] Gide's journals are rich with references to Blanche Monnier compared to their relative silence about Marcel Redureau, for example. A number of people in Gide's circle were isolated or confined, and his evocations of their lives sometimes echo elements of *La Séquestrée*. A 1914 visit to his former piano teacher Marc de La Nux (1830–1914)—whose name is changed to La

---

43. André Gide, *Correspondance (1910–1936), André Gide–Jean-Richard Bloch*, ed. Bernard Duchatelet (Brest, France: Centre d'étude des correspondances et journaux intimes des XIXe et XXe siècles, CNRS [UMR 6563]—Faculté des lettres Victor Ségalen, 1997), 115 (letter dated November 14, 192).

44. André Gide, *Correspondance, 1927–1950, André Gide–Thea Sternheim*, ed. Claude Foucart (Bron, France: Centre d'études gidiennes, Université Lyon II, 1986), 28 (letter dated March 2, 1933) and 41 (letter dated August 1, 1939).

45. George Painter, *André Gide: A Critical and Biographical Study* (London: A. Barker, 1951), 108.

Pérouse in the *Journal*—is one case. Gide offers a detailed description of the squalor in de La Nux's room, where he was confined by illness. The pathos in an inventory of miserable objects belonging to an unkempt life is similar, although not as extreme, to that of Blanche's world. Another confined friend was Marcel Proust, who by 1921 was mostly bedridden. Ever an observer of pathologies, Gide describes Proust's stiffly rubbing his nose with "the gesture of an animal or a madman."[46]

As Gide's pious wife Madeleine became more extreme in her self-abnegation and isolation at her family estate of Cuverville, she seemed to turn into a different kind of prisoner, obsessed with doing good works. In wartime exile in Algeria, the elderly Gide returned to phrases from *Séquestrée* to describe his own experiences. In January 1943 he wrote in his journal about an old Algerian woman who slept in what she called her "little storeroom." which reminded him of the way Blanche Monnier spoke of her "dear great back-Malampia." Four months later Gide reflected that he no longer enjoyed taking strolls and was "pleased to return to [his] grotto," another term that Blanche used for her room.[47]

⚜ ⚜ ⚜

All the texts in *Ne jugez pas* were assembled from a "need to *bear witness.*" Gide did not overvalue these productions as writing per se, stating that *Souvenirs de la cour d'assises* bore "almost no relation to literature."[48] Yet they are closely related to Gide, his ideals, and his sense of a writer's role in society. They deserve to be more widely known, and it is hoped that the present English translation will help make this possible.

⚜ ⚜ ⚜

I would like to thank the University of Illinois Press's inspired team, especially its director, Willis Regier, and Bruce Bethell, manuscript editor.

For inspiration and advice, thanks go to Richard Howard, Marie Ponsot, Jacques Drillon, Wojciech Karpinski, Harold Rolfe, and Boonkhet Hangsuwan.

46. Gide, *Journals,* 2:63 (entry for August 15, 1914) and 2:267 (entries for May 15–28, 1921).
47. Ibid., 4:155 (entry for January 14, 1943) and 4:208 (entry for May 1, 1943).
48. Ibid., 4:288.

Judge Not

❦ ❦ ❦ A Memoir of the Assize Court

(Rouen, May 1912)

I've always felt an irresistible fascination for tribunals. When I travel, four things attract me most of all in a city—the municipal park, marketplace, cemetery, and courthouse.

Now I know from experience that it's an entirely different thing to hear justice done and to help to do it oneself. When one is among the onlookers, one can still believe in it. Seated in the jury box, one repeats Christ's saying, "Judge not."

Of course, I don't believe that society can do without tribunals and judges. But over the course of twelve days, I could feel with anguish how doubtful and precarious a thing is human justice. To some extent, this may still be reflected in these notes.

Nevertheless, I wish to state here from the outset, to temper somewhat the criticisms that occur in my narratives, that what struck me most during the sessions was the conscientiousness with which everyone—judges, lawyers, and jurors—carried out his duties. More than once I truly admired the assize court president's alertness and knowledge of every case;[1] the urgency of his cross-examinations; the plaintiffs' decisiveness and restraint; defense counsels' concise speeches, free of useless eloquence; and finally, the jurors' attentiveness. I confess that all this exceeded my expectations, but it made some of the machine's creakings all the more frightening.

No doubt certain reforms might be gradually introduced, involving

---

1. Tr. note: In France the criminal courts distinguish three types of offenses: petty offenses, tried by police courts; misdemeanors, tried by criminal courts; and serious indictable offenses or crimes, tried by the assize court—the only court with lay jurors and from which there is no appeal against sentences (source: *Profile of France,* published by the French Ministry of Foreign Affairs). The assize court has more than one judge; the president is thus the presiding judge.

judges and cross-examination, as well as jurors.[2] It is not my purpose here to suggest them.

Chapter 1

Monday (May 1912)

We proceeded to the choice of jurors: a notary, an architect, and a retired schoolteacher. All the rest were recruited from among shopkeepers, tradesmen, laborers, farmers, and modest landlords. One of them could barely write, and on his voting ballot it would be difficult to tell a yes from a no. But apart from two people who didn't give a hang about anything and kept getting themselves excused anyway, everyone seemed determined to apply his full conscience and awareness.

The farmers, distinctly in the majority, were resolved to be very strict. The exploits of tragic thieves like Bonnot[3] and others have been in the public eye recently, and the watchword, prompted by the newspapers, was now "Show no mercy!"; the gentlemen of the jury represented *Society* and were resolved to defend it.

One of the jurors was missing. No letter of excuse was received from him, and there was no reason for his absence; he was fined the statutory amount—three hundred francs, I believe. We were already drawing names to see who would sit on the first case when the defaulting juror turned up, drenched in sweat; he was a poor old farmer right out of Labiche's *La Cagnotte*.[4] Loud laughter broke out when he explained that he had been circling the courthouse for a half-hour, unable to find the entrance. The fine was withdrawn.

From an absurd fear of making myself conspicuous, I didn't take any notes on the first case, an indecent assault (we would judge five such cases); the accused was acquitted, not because there was any doubt of

2. On this subject, see a report in *Le Temps,* the October 13 issue, pp. 14 ff., and *L'Opinion,* the issues of October 18 and 25, 1912.

3. Tr. note: Jules Bonnot (1876–1912) was a French criminal who pioneered the use of automobiles in robberies; known as "The Tragic Bandit," he inspired sympathy for his anarchist and prolabor beliefs and was killed in a gun battle with French police.

4. Tr. note: *La Cagnotte* (1864), a comedy by playwright Eugène Labiche (1815–88), makes fun of provincial tourists in Paris.

his guilt, but because the jurors didn't think it worth punishing him for such a minor offense. I wasn't on the jury for that case, but between sessions I overheard conversations among those who were. Some were indignant that the court should be involved with such trifles, of the sort committed—as they expressed it—every day and all over.

I don't know how they managed to obtain an acquittal while admitting the individual was guilty of the acts in question. The majority must have, quite untruthfully, written "no" on the ballot in response to the question, "Is X guilty, etc. . . . ?" We would experience this situation repeatedly, and I will later dwell on another such case in which I served on the jury and witnessed the upset, even anguish, of some jurors faced with a questionnaire so conceived that they were forced to vote against the truth to obtain what they saw as justice.

⚘ ⚘ ⚘

On the same day, the second case brought me to the jury box and put the defendants Alphonse and Arthur before me.

Arthur was a young swindler with a high forehead and thin mustache, looking somewhat flabbergasted, a bit like a Daumier.[5] He said that he worked as a shop assistant for a certain Monsieur X——, but a report showed that Monsieur X—— does not own a shop.

Alphonse was a "sales representative." Dressed in a nut-brown overcoat with wide lapels in darker silk, he had dark brown plastered-down hair, a red face, glazed eyes, a heavy mustache, and an arrogant, roguish appearance. Thirty years old, he lived in Le Havre with Arthur's sister; the two brothers-in-law had been intimately associated for a long time, and both were under indictment.

The case was rather muddled. First, it involved the theft of a large quantity of furs and then a burglary with no result—apart from mayhem, the cutting of a tobacco pouch valued at three francs, and a useless checkbook. The first theft could not be reconstituted, and the charges remained so vague that the indictment focused instead on the second. But there was nothing specific here either, just a collection of small facts, conjectures, and deductions.

---

5. Tr. note: The French painter, caricaturist, and sculptor Honoré Daumier (1808–79) created a series of images satirizing the French legal system.

The uncertain indictment associated the two defendants, but their defense methods differed. Alphonse put on a good face, with a cultivated air, and laughed wittily at some of the remarks made by the president of the court of assize:

"You smoked big cigars."

"Oh," he said disdainfully, "they were twenty-five-centime Havanas!"

"That's not exactly what you said during the preliminary investigation," said the president a little later. "Why haven't you persisted in your denials?"

"Because I saw that it would cause me problems," he answered, laughing.

He was perfectly self-possessed and doled out his statements skillfully. His job as "traveling salesman" remained highly dubious. He was said to be the "lover" of a sixty-year-old spinster. He protested, "She's a mother to me."

The effect on the jury was lamentable. Did he realize it? Gradually, his forehead began to glisten.

Arthur was scarcely more sympathetic. The jury's opinion was that after all, if it wasn't certain that they committed *these specific thefts*, they must have committed other ones, or they would commit others in future, and that therefore they should be put behind bars.

However, they could be convicted only of *this* specific theft.

"How could I have done it?" asked Arthur. "I wasn't in Le Havre that day."

But pieces of a postcard in his handwriting postmarked at Le Havre on October 30, the day of the theft, were confiscated in his mistress's room.

This is how Arthur defended himself:

"That day," he said, more or less, "I sent my mistress not one card but *two*; as their pictures were 'a little naughty' (in fact, they showed Adam and Eve from the Rouen Cathedral), I slipped them, picture against picture, into a single clear envelope after having written the address twice and stamped them both, and tore the envelopes in the place where the stamps were pasted, in order to let them both be canceled. When it was mailed, no doubt only one of the stamps was canceled. When it got to Le Havre, the postal employee there canceled the other one. That's why it was postmarked Le Havre."[6]

At least that's what I managed to untangle from his confused protests, rattled by a president whose mind was made up and who seemed quite determined to hear nothing new. I had the greatest difficulty in understanding and even hearing what Arthur was saying, because he was constantly interrupted and finally just spluttered. The jury gave up trying to listen to him, for he didn't manage to interest them.

Yet his explanation held together, especially since it is doubtful that a swindler as skilled as Arthur seemed to be would have left behind— or rather created—this kind of incriminating evidence on the night of a crime. Moreover, if he himself was in Le Havre, what need would there have been to write to his mistress in Le Havre, when he simply could have gone to see her?

I know that jurors have the right, if not exactly to intervene in the proceedings, at least to speak to the president and ask that a certain question be put to a defendant or witness if they feel it will shed light on the proceedings or their personal suspicions, which they neverthe-less must not reveal. Did I dare use this prerogative? It's hard to imag-ine how unsettling it is to rise up and speak in front of the court. If I ever had to "testify," I would surely lose my composure, and what would I feel in the defendant's box? The proceedings were almost over, with only a moment left. I summoned all my courage, realizing that if

6. Tr. note: This detailed argument involving the French postal system confused even one of Gide's editors at Gallimard in the 1930s. In 1912, sending a letter cost ten centimes. The defendant had put two postcards, with images facing inward, into a single clear envelope. He then cut off bits of the envelope to let the post office cancel the stamps on the postcards, inside the envelope. There were two five centime stamps, one on each card. Usually a stamp was canceled when it was mailed. However, the defendant claimed that the postal employee, see-ing that one of the two stamps had not been canceled when the letter arrived, canceled it belatedly, so that the stamp could not be reused later. Gide was interested to find out whether the stamp in question, which he had not seen, was for five or ten centimes. If it was a stamp for ten centimes, then the defendant lied. If it was for five centimes, then he might indeed have sent two cards, each stamped with five centimes, which would explain why one of the cards was canceled when it arrived. Most important, it could not be used as evidence that the defendant was necessarily in Le Havre just because the card was postmarked Le Havre. That's why, when Gide saw that the second stamp was for ten centimes, his suspicions were not confirmed. I am indebted for Gidean and philatelic information in this note to the French poet and translator Jacques Drillon.

I didn't overcome my timidity this time, the chance would be missed for the rest of the session. I asked haltingly:

"Could the president ask the postal worker who just testified if the cancellation at the starting point is different from the one made when the letter arrives?"

For indeed, were it possible to discern that the stamp had been canceled on arrival, as Arthur claimed, rather than when it was sent, as the prosecution claimed, what would remain of the latter's case?

The president, not having followed Arthur's muddled arguments, clearly didn't understand the meaning of my question; still, he obligingly recalled the witness:

"You've heard the question from the gentleman of the jury? Kindly respond to it."

The employee launched into a profuse explanation meant to prove that since the times when letters go out are not the same as the times when they come in, there was no way to confuse the two. Moreover, outgoing and incoming letters are not postmarked in the same office, and so on. However, he did not address the only matter that interested me, about which we knew no more than before: whether one could definitively identify from the postcard fragment whether the postmark was made when the letter was sent out or received. Yet the witness had completed his *explanation*.

"Monsieur juror, are you satisfied?"

I tried to formulate a new question that was more exacting than my first one. Could I say that no, I was not satisfied, that the witness hadn't answered my question at all? Moreover, I felt that neither any of the jurors nor the president had understood my question. At least none of the jurors understood why I asked it. No one could follow Arthur's arguments, which I myself followed only with considerable effort. He had a nasty face, clumsy physique, and unpleasant voice; he was unable to make himself heard. Opinions were formed, and even if we were now to discover that the postcard was not from him . . .

The prosecution and defense rested their cases.

A bit later, in the jury room.

The jurors are unanimous, resolutely deciding against the two defendants, without qualification, and refusing to see any difference between the two. Clearly they were swindlers, brigands in the making, only waiting for the opportunity to use a revolver or truncheon (perhaps they were too refined to use a knife). Nevertheless, no incontrovertible evidence of their guilt in the two thefts of which they were accused had been put forward, apart from the identification of a few connections—which they called coincidences. Nothing absolutely decisive in the indictment convinced the jury. They were surely guilty, but perhaps not of these crimes. Was it plausible or even possible that Alphonse could have lugged a huge bundle estimated at a meter wide by two meters high around Trouville, where he was well known, in the crowded rue de Paris at an early hour and not have been noticed by anyone? That was the first theft, a theft of the furs.

Finally, although they were swindlers, they weren't really *brigands*. I mean that they *profited* from society but did not rebel against it. They wanted to benefit themselves, not hurt others, and so on. That's what the jurors told themselves, aiming for a measured strictness. In short, they agreed to convict, but in a limited way: guilt was recognized without any extenuating circumstances but also without aggravating circumstances. These depended on the following questions: Was the robbery committed *during the night? . . . by several people? . . . in an inhabited building? . . . with duplicated keys or by breaking and entering?*

As it was obvious that the robbery had been committed, and could not have been done otherwise, the jurors naturally were obliged to reply yes to each question, *despite what they had previously decided.*

"But gentlemen," said one of the jurors (the youngest and the only one who seemed to have some rudiments of education), "saying no to these questions doesn't mean that you believe there was no break-in, that it didn't happen at night, and so on. It just means that you don't wish to retain that count of the indictment."

His reasoning went over their heads.

"We don't need to get into that," one replied. "We just have to answer the question. Monsieur Foreman, please read it again."

"Was the burglary committed at night?"

"Can't say no to that," others replied.

Even though some no votes were found in the ballot box, yes votes were in the vast majority.

In this way all those who had decided to vote just *guilty*, but without extenuating or aggravating circumstances, found themselves voting for the extenuations in order to *compensate* for the excess of aggravations that the arguments had forced them to accept.

Immediately afterward, voices were raised:

"Ah, here's a fine mess! It's a disgrace! They won't be punished enough! Extenuating circumstances—imagine that! If only they'd let us vote them just plain *guilty*!"

To everyone's relief, the court levied a fairly long sentence (six years' imprisonment and a ten-year exile), paying as little attention as possible to the jury's verdict.

I've noted in some detail the perplexity and upset that governed the jury room. I found them to be nearly identical at every deliberation. The questions were asked in such a way as rarely to allow the juror to vote as he might wish, the way he felt would be fair. I will return to this question later.

As I left this first session, I felt dissatisfied. I almost rejoiced that Arthur seemed so unsympathetic to me, for otherwise I wouldn't have been able to sleep that night. No matter! It seemed monstrous not to heed his defense. The more I thought about it, the more plausible it seemed to me . . . That's when I got the idea (why hadn't it occurred to me before?) that if Arthur's postcard or, at least in his version of the events, the two paired cards were stamped on both sides of the envelope, each of the stamps need be for only five centimes. Therefore, if the stamp on the recovered fragment of a card was for five centimes, then it could not be the only one. A ten-centime stamp might not prove that Arthur was wrong, for perhaps he put the two cards into the same envelope after having stamped them. But a five-centime stamp would surely prove that he was right. I resolved to ask the district attorney, whom I fortunately know, for permission to examine the little piece of paper in Arthur's file.

‡ ‡ ‡

Tuesday

When I passed in front of the caretaker's office, he stopped me and handed over a letter. It was sent from prison by Arthur. How did he get my name? From his lawyer, surely.

The question that I asked during the cross-examination must have convinced him that I took an interest in him, that I doubted he was guilty, and perhaps I would help him . . .

He begged me to use my right to ask to visit him in his cell, saying that he had some important things to explain to me and so on.

First I would look at his file. If the bit of postcard was inadequately stamped, I would share my doubts with the district attorney.

After the session I was able to see the file. The postcard had a ten-centime stamp, so I gave up.

Yet I tell myself today that if each stamp had been for five centimes, the postal worker would have canceled both of them straightaway. On the contrary, if the stamp on a single side were sufficient in itself, then the other stamp might have escaped him and been canceled only when the letter arrived . . .

Chapter 2

The second day, too, began with a "vice matter." The president ordered the case to be heard in camera. For the first time, applying a recent circular from the lord chancellor, the soldiers on duty had to leave, to their obvious displeasure. "*Their presence*," the worthy circular read, "*in any case hardly seems indispensable most of the time, for as the courtroom is empty, police constables provide a sufficient guard for the defendant.*"

Ah, if only the children could have left, too! Alas, their testimony was necessary. First the little girl who had been raped, and then her ten-year-old brother, a little older than she. Have mercy, Monsieur President, and make the cross-examinations a bit shorter! Why must we dwell on it, since the facts have already been admitted, the doctor has made the necessary observations, and the defendant has confessed to everything? The unfortunate man! There he was, dressed in rags, ugly, sickly, with a shaved head and already looking like a forced laborer. At twenty years old, he was so puny that he barely looked pubescent. He held a paper in his hand (I thought that this was forbidden), a paper covered with writing, that he read and reread anxiously. No doubt he was trying to learn by heart the answers that his lawyer had suggested.

Some disgraceful information was heard about him: he associated with habitual criminals and haunted cabarets of ill repute. His jail record consisted of eight days for breach of trust and, shortly thereafter, a month for theft. Now he is accused of having "completely violated" the little girl Y. D., seven years old.

. . . .

The president continued in an even tone of practically gentle reproach, which was much appreciated by the jurors:

"Well, my boy, what you did wasn't a good thing!"

"I see that pretty well m'self."

"Have you anything to add? Any regrets to express?"

"No, Monsieur President."

It's clear to me that the defendant did not understand the second question or that he meant to answer only the first one. Nevertheless, an indignant murmur went through the jury box and continued as far as the lawyers' bench.

Just then the defense attorney asked whether the defendant was interned in a poorhouse eleven years before. This was acknowledged.

Witnesses were called. First, the little girl's mother, but she saw nothing, and the only thing she could say was that, returning home from work, she found her little girl in the street crying, and at first she gave her two slaps.

Now it was the child's turn.[7] She was clean and well-behaved, but we could see that the apparatus of justice—the boxes, the solemnity, the kind of throne where three oddly dressed old men sit—all of it terrified her.

7. The day before we had already seen a child testify; a little girl, about the same age as this one, also joined by her mother. But in that case their appearance surely argued in favor of the defendant and I imagine contributed greatly to his acquittal. The mother looked like a madam, and while the accused sobbed with shame from the defendant's box, the "victim" moved very resolutely toward the judge. Since she had her back to the court, I couldn't see her face, but the first words the president said to her, before having the little one climb onto a chair to bring her closer to his ear—"See here! Don't laugh, my child"—informed the jury clearly enough.

There was more:

"You screamed?"

"No, sir."

"Why did you say during cross-examination that you screamed?"

"'Cause I made a mistake."

"See here, don't be afraid, my child; come closer."

As they had yesterday, they made the little girl climb onto a chair so that she reached the level of the court and the president could hear her answers. He immediately repeated them aloud for the jurors' edification. We saw the little girl from behind. She was trembling, and this time it wasn't laughter but sobs that shook her. She pulled a handkerchief from the pocket of her smock.

The cross-examination was horrible, and how useless it was to dwell on what he did to her, since we already knew it quite thoroughly. Moreover, the little girl was *unable* to reply, except in monosyllables.

The child's voice was so weak that the president leaned over to hear her, cupping his hand to his ear. Then he sat up and turned to the jury.

. . . . [8]

The lawyer for this dismal case had neglected to summon witnesses for the defense in time. By virtue of the president's discretionary powers, however, we nevertheless heard testimony from Madame X——, a poor street vendor who seemed to have adopted the unfortunate person, because, she stated, "His sister had a baby with my son."

Madame X—— had a purplish-blue complexion and a neck as wide as a person's thigh. A bonnet with strings perched on her pulled-back, slicked-down hair, which receded around the ears. A deep line furrowed her forehead, and her left hand, in a sling, was wrapped in rags. She was crying. In a pathetic voice, she pled for mercy for the poor boy, "who never knew happiness." She described him as the son of alcoholics who continually beat him at home: "They made him sleep in the bathroom." A mere glance at him showed that he remained a child. He plays with pictures, marbles, and a top. But he had already attempted to "lie on top of the little one," who bit him on the ear at the time. He wrote incoherent letters from prison to the vegetable seller. The worthy woman pulled a bundle of papers from her pocket and sobbed.

The cross-examination was finished. The unfortunate man made strenuous efforts to follow the district attorney's speech for the prosecution, of which he clearly could understand just a few sentences here

---

8. The complete text of the in camera session was provided in a separate printing (in seventy copies) of the first edition.

and there. But soon he would understand very well that he was sentenced to eight years in prison.

Meanwhile the president informed us that according to the defendant's admission during cross-examination, "this was the first time that he had sexual intercourse." So that's all he will have known of "love"!

❦ ❦ ❦

The second case of the second day brought to the defendant's box a twenty-year-old boy with a gentle appearance, slightly depressed but harmless. Marceau lost his mother at age four, never knew his father, and was raised in an orphanage. Before he was sixteen he had already held two jobs as a mechanic. Accused of theft, he was sentenced to six months in prison by the Yvetot court, as the Berenger Law allows.[9]

After the conviction he was fired by his employer, the mechanic. Since then he still worked, but randomly, often changing bosses, switching from farmhand to longshoreman to mechanic. His employers were satisfied with him, although they did find his personality "a little gloomy." Emboldened by my question the day before, I ventured to ask the president what the witness meant by that.

The witness: "I mean that he kept to himself and never went out to drink or have fun with the others."

At that time Marceau owed:

Forty-five francs to a bicycle vendor.

Seventy francs to a launderer.

Seven francs to a shoemaker.

With such low wages, *how could he ever pay them back, without stealing?*

His first theft had already been committed "with premeditation." We learn that on the previous Sunday, he bought a candle. Then, the day before the theft, he borrowed a screwdriver from his boss to open a drawer in which he discovered and took the thirty-five francs.

---

9. Tr. note: The Berenger Law, which passed in March 1891, was written by Senator Henri Berenger (1830–1915) and introduced to the French judiciary the possibility of a suspended sentence.

The crime we dealt with today required more skillful preparation. At least, a first failed attempt served as a sort of dress rehearsal.

The night of March 26 was the first time that Marceau broke into the lonely little house at ———— in which old Madame Prune, a restaurant owner, and her maid lived. On the ground floor he broke a windowpane in the dining room, opened the window, and came into the room. He confessed that he had hoped to find money in a kitchen drawer. But the kitchen door was locked, and after a few failed attempts to open it, he left, planning to return the next day with better equipment.

On the afternoon of March 27, suspecting that the broken windowpane might have raised an alarm, Marceau climbed onto his bicycle and returned to ————, when he spied part of a horseshoe on the road. He picked it up, thinking that it might prove useful. I forgot to say that the night before, he equipped himself with a candle, purchased at Grainville. In this way Marceau prowled around the house, making sure that everything was quiet, and somehow convinced himself that no one suspected anything—which was true.

The defendant's cross-examination reconstructed the crime. Marceau didn't try to defend himself or even apologize. He admitted doing what he did, as if he were unable to avoid it. One might say he was resigned beforehand to becoming a criminal.

Therefore, on the night of the twenty-seventh, there he was at ————, at the given time. The window into which he had climbed the night before remained open, and he went through it into the dining room. But that night, as his intentions were serious, he carefully closed the shutters behind him. He held a bicycle lamp in his hand, a lamp without a base that couldn't be put down, which was inconvenient. Soon, in the kitchen, he exchanged it for a candlestick and pried open the door with the horseshoe. Then he rummaged around the drawers. Eleven *sous*! That wasn't worth stopping for. He would collect them later, on his way back. He went up to the second floor.

Madame Prune and her maid occupied the first two rooms, to the right of the landing on the second floor. Travelers were sometimes lodged in the two rooms to the left. Marceau quietly checked to see that the latter rooms were empty; he held a short, sharp-pointed knife that he had found in a kitchen drawer.

President: "Why did you take that knife?"

Marceau: "To let the maid have it."

But her door was locked. Marceau labored to open it, but hearing noise coming from the old woman's room, he ran to hide in one of the empty rooms. He blew out the candle, and as he knelt to put the candlestick on the floor, the knife, which he had slipped into his jacket, happened to fall. He was unable to find it in the dark. When he emerged into the hallway, he faced the old woman unarmed, fortunately for both of them.

Madame Prune came up to testify in turn. She was a dignified and frail little old woman of eighty-one. Barely able to stand, she requested a chair, which was brought to her and on which she sat, next to the witness box.

"So I heard a creaking noise in my house. I said to myself, 'My God, what's that? I hear creaking. Could it be hail?' I got up and opened the window that looks out on the backyard, but I couldn't see anything. I went back to bed. Then the creaking started again. I got up again. Again nothing. I went back to bed. My clock said midnight. Then I saw light from under my door. 'Oh!' I said, 'I hope it isn't a fire.' I called my maid, but she didn't come. 'All the same,' I told myself, *'time was, I used to be braver.'* And I went out into the hallway to my maid's door, calling, 'There be thieves in the house, my poor girl, ah! My God! There be thieves in the house!' She didn't reply, and her door was closed."

That's when Marceau, returning to the hallway, threw himself on the old woman, who was easy to knock over.

"Why did you grab Madame Prune by the neck?"

"To strangle her."

He said it without bragging or unease, as openly as the president had posed the question.

Loud laughter was heard from the crowd.

District attorney: "The spectators' behavior is inexplicable and indecent."

President: "You're quite right. Gentlemen, reflect that the case we are judging here is highly serious, of the sort to bring a sentence of capital punishment for the defendant if there are no extenuating circumstances."

Meanwhile the maid called for help from the window. A neighbor replied: "We're coming! We're coming!" Hearing them arrive, the young man ran away terrified, leaving his crime unfinished.

The court sentenced Marceau to eight years of hard labor.

On several occasions I noticed that Marceau looked particularly uneasy whenever he felt that the *reconstruction* of his crime was not totally exact, although he could neither correct the account nor *benefit from any inaccuracies.* That's what I found oddest about this case.

⚜ ⚜ ⚜

On the same day we tried an arsonist.

Bernard was a day laborer, forty years old, with a jolly appearance and a round head. He was bald but made up for that by his mustache. He wore a soft striped shirt and a tie to attempt to hide a filthy collar. He clutched a threadbare cap in his hands. Bernard had no criminal record. The information available about him was not negative. All that was found to say about him was that his personality was "underhanded." He was never seen in bars, but some people claimed that he "drank at home." Nevertheless, he had his wits about him. It was said that his father, a respected village policeman, "took to drink" and that both of his brothers were "out-and-out alcoholics."

Bernard was accused of setting four fires. First, the winepress of his sister-in-law, the widow Bernard, was set afire on December 30, 1911.

President: "Who set the fire?"

Defendant: "I did, Your Honor."

President: "How did you set it?"

Defendant: "With a match."

President: "Why did you set it?"

Defendant: "I had no reasons."

President: "Were you drinking that night?"

Defendant: "No, Your Honor."

President: "Did you ever argue with your sister-in-law?"

Defendant: "Never, Your Honor. We got along fine."

President: "You returned at 7:30 from your boss's place. What did you do until 9:30?"

Defendant: "I read the newspaper."

On January 1—that is to say, two days later—it was the turn of his sister-in-law's house.

The president wanted to establish that Bernard was drunk that night and insisted that he confess to the fact. Bernard protested that he had had nothing to drink.

On the evening of January 1, a holiday, his family had gathered, with cousins, nephews, and so on. Bernard refused to dine with them and left at 6:30. During the conversation at table, when they spoke about the fire of two days before, they recalled having heard him say that there would soon be more.

The same night fire broke out at the widow Bernard's home, and the neighbors called him, shouting, "Fire! Help!" Although he was the closest neighbor and relative, he shut his door and reappeared a only quarter of an hour later. Moreover, he did not attempt to deny anything. He had started the second fire as well as the first, and the two others that would follow.

President: "So you don't want to say why you set them?"

Defendant: "Your Honor, I've told you that I had no reasons."

"It's truly disturbing that he has this inclination," said the widow. "Otherwise we had no complaint about his work."

Called to testify, the sworn-in doctor told us of the odd relief and relaxation that Bernard told him he felt after having set the fire.

Moreover, he confessed to him that he hadn't felt the same relaxation after the next fires, "so that he missed it."

I would like to have known whether this strange satisfaction in setting fires and this relaxation was related to the sexual climax, but even though I was on the jury, I didn't dare ask the question, fearing that it might seem absurd.

Chapter 3

Wednesday

Another indecent assault, committed by a day laborer from Barentin. The father of five children, of whom the eldest is twelve years old, assaulted his own daughter. An in camera hearing was requested.

When the public was readmitted into the room, an indignant murmur greeted the jury's decision and its desire to recognize extenuating circumstances.

I myself was rather surprised (as I had been in previous cases of this type) to see the moderation that the majority of jurors brought to it. In the jury room, much was made of the fact that the assault did not include violence. Finally and above all, the defendant's wife showed such a strong, if unconscious, desire to get rid of her husband, and the passion that she could not keep out of her testimony considerably lessened its weight. The defendant also benefited from the lack of sympathy that we could accord the victim. That's what the public could not know after the in camera sessions. To some jurors, even a five-year prison sentence seemed excessive. By contrast, all approved of the withdrawal of parental rights.

The defendant heard the sentence of five years without flinching, but on hearing the loss of parental status, he gave a sort of strange howl, like an animal's protest, a cry composed of revolt, shame, and grief.

The strange case that came next brought before us a head clerk from the receiver's office of the postal service (the Rouen central office).

He was a large, thick, red-faced man with square shoulders and no neck. His hands were brutish, and he wore a low collar with a thin gray tie. His hair was cropped short over a low forehead. Forty-seven years old, he had fought in the Madagascar campaign, where he had picked up malarial fever. He was prone to drinking binges and had experienced a few hallucinations, so that a medical report noted his diminished responsibility. But since he started working for the post office, his conduct had been irreproachable. And he was quite sober on the morning of April 2, when he removed from the office an envelope containing 13,000 francs. He admitted the facts, apologized, and didn't even try to explain. Every day he was required to handle considerable amounts. That very morning, beside the envelope with 13,000 francs, *there was another envelope containing 15,000 francs, just as accessible, that he saw but did not take.*

But he quickly put the envelope with 13,000 francs into his pocket. He left the loading dock, telling a colleague that he was going to the toilet, and calmly took his overcoat and hat. Because it was 12:30, no one was surprised to see him leave. Outside he didn't run or hide from anyone but went to a nearby brothel, spent 246 francs to treat the house, and then awoke, sheepish. He returned the remainder of the money to the management, promising to pay back the difference.

The jury brought in a negative verdict, and the court acquitted him.

Chapter 4

Thursday

The young woman Rachel is accused of infanticide.

She moves fearfully up to the bar, wearing a white woolen shawl over a black blouse. From where I sit, I can't see her face clearly, and her voice is soft. She is a servant in Saint-Martin-de-B. and has been in the same house since the age of thirteen. Now she is seventeen.

She had managed to conceal her pregnancy; the first pains came to her while she was milking the cows. She went inside and poured the milk in the dairy, and then she cleaned house, but the pains became so strong that she had to sit down. She was frightfully pale.

"If you're sick, go up and rest in your room," said her employer.

Bertha Rachel's room was on the second floor, next to the master's. As soon as she stretched out on the straw mattress, she gave birth to a little girl.

She was "afraid of being scolded," and since the little one was crying, Bertha put her hand over the baby's mouth and kept it there until the crying stopped, out of fear that her boss might hear. When Bertha saw that the child was no longer breathing, she took a pair of scissors from her skirt and stabbed her throat superficially.

It emerged from the cross-examination that she stabbed with the scissors only after the baby was already dead of suffocation. The prosecutor tried to establish that this was "to prove that the blood had stopped circulating." I believe it was more unthinking than that. The president questioned Bertha ardently, but the role of the scissors remained no less murky.

When Bertha Rachel was certain that her child was no longer alive, she temporarily hid the tiny corpse in a wash bucket, threw the placenta out the window, which was directly over the dung heap, and immediately went downstairs, back to work.

The next day she dug a hole behind the barn with a peat spade, at the edge of a ditch—a shallow hole, since she was exhausted—where she buried the child.

The police were notified a few days later by an anonymous letter, and the child's corpse was found. The president did not feel obliged to dwell on the anonymous letter, about which no information was given. I wasn't on the jury for this case, so that no question was asked about the subject, and they moved on.

President: "During your pregnancy, did your employer suspect anything?"

Defendant: "They surely saw that I was getting fatter, but my mistress didn't want to say it. She didn't say anything at all to me about it."

Then suddenly, in a lower voice, somewhat abashedly:

"It's the boss's son who did it to me."

President: "You didn't mention that before."

Then, turning to the jury: "In the preliminary investigation, she stubbornly refused to say who the child's father was."

The young woman Rachel continued, without listening to the judge:

"He told me to make it disappear so no one would know it was his."

President: "Make it disappear how?"

"By puttin' it underground."

This was said in a perfectly toneless voice. The poor girl appeared to be an idiot.

President: "As the defendant said nothing about this at the preliminary investigation, we cannot call as witness the man she is speaking of now." To the defendant: "You may sit down."

Just then the defense attorney stood up:

"It's unfortunate that the defendant didn't speak to us here as she did in the preliminary investigation, of her family at the farm, reading aloud in the evening. They would read news items, and the older relatives who did the reading liked to emphasize the stories about infanticide, she said."

President: "Counselor X——, I don't really see how this can be relevant."

Too bad! Fortunately, the jurors saw the relevance quite plainly. The whole matter became clearer when the employer came to the witness box—an old woman of over sixty, gaunt and rigid as if mummified, with hard features, cold eyes, and pursed lips. Her face was shadowed by a black lace bonnet, and the ribbon that tied it hung over a short black cape.

President: "The young woman Rachel was in your employ? Were you pleased with her?"

Employer: "Oh! Yes, I was quite pleased with her. For sure, I had no complaints about her."

President: "You never noticed that she was pregnant?"

Employer: "No, never. If I'd known of her condition, I would have let her go, for sure."

President: "In the preliminary investigation you said that you saw quite clearly that she was becoming *grandiose,* but you thought it was a stomach problem. The day before she gave birth, you saw blood and water in the kitchen, at a place where the girl had been sitting."

Employer: "I thought it came from a chicken that had just been cleaned."

One sensed even more from the old woman's flat, dry voice her will to know nothing, to have seen nothing, and to continue to see nothing.

The preliminary investigation revealed that no men ever visited the remote farm and that the girl could have seen only her employer's husband, aged seventy-five, or the son, aged thirty-two, in one of his rare, brief appearances. The old woman also informed us that the servant's room was accessible only through her own room, mentioned to prove that it could not be her son who . . . and so on.

The president, clearly wanting to keep the case on course and to limit the indictments, moved on.

The doctor's testimony did not inform us of anything new. He explained at great length that the child was born alive, so this was a case of infanticide, not abortion. The scissors stab, superficial and somewhat tentative, was meant to verify that the child was dead. But it had indeed once breathed, for bits of pulmonary residue floated in the bucket of water into which she had put it.

While the jury deliberated, a murmur went around the court. The employer's son was pointed out in the court, sitting next to his mother. Bothered by the hostile glances, he kept his head down, leaning against the knob of his cane, and I didn't manage to see him.

The young woman Rachel was found guilty, but because she acted without proper judgment, she was acquitted and sent home to her parents.

❦ ❦ ❦

Prosper, a tailor born in '86 at X—— and whose nickname was Bouboule, was brought before us.

He looked extraordinarily like a pencil pusher, with a vast bulging forehead and long straight hair parted in the middle. Despite his general thickness of torso and limbs, he had small hands, with wide but short fingers that seemed to be missing a joint. The prison outfit he wore accentuated his fat, hunched-up appearance. The juror to my right leaned over to me and said: "He doesn't look smart!"

My neighbor on the left answered quietly: "He doesn't look stupid!"

From age ten to fourteen he was convicted four times for theft. After being remanded three times to his parents' custody, he was finally sent to prison, where he remained until adulthood, subject to special surveillance.

He had been indicted five times since first being set free. From age twenty to twenty-four, he worked at D——, where he found Bègue, a former comrade from prison; they would work together, always together. Each time they burglarized a home, they left the remains of an impromptu banquet in the kitchen; there would be empty bottles and used glasses on the table, as well as turds on the living-room rug. Each time, they didn't just steal but left behind as much damage as possible. In one house where they couldn't find any cash, they left a prominently displayed lid from a box of starch with these words scrawled in Bègue's handwriting: "Should have left money, you bunch of pigs."

Exactly six months before our day in court, Bègue was given a life sentence at hard labor for having burgled several houses at N—— and P—— "in violent circumstances that particularly aggravated the case," the press reported. At this moment one of the defendants, Prosper, was still missing. He was arrested three months later at Y——, where he was hiding after extensive wanderings around Spain.

It seems that Bègue confessed to everything. By contrast, Prosper denied everything, claiming to be the victim of an error, framed for his resemblance to Bouboule—since Bouboule, he claimed, was not him. This statement provoked loud laughter in the court.

Even though I was not convinced by this, I would like to have followed his defense a bit more closely, but the president rushed through, not allowing Bouboule—or Prosper—the time to explain himself.

Once again I felt, not without anguish, how much a president could hinder or facilitate testimony (even unconsciously) and how hard it was for a jury to develop its own opinion rather than simply adopt the president's.[10]

Prosper spoke in a muffled voice that was rather difficult to hear, and he seemed to have great trouble expressing himself. During the cross-examination, feeling the net tightening around him, he said that fate was persecuting him and spoke of a "conspiracy." He grew pale, and fat drops of sweat started to roll down his forehead.

Called as a witness, the gatekeeper at one of the burgled homes, Monsieur X——, gave very moving and fine testimony. His self-possession and courage, as well as his modest manner, were admirable.

10. I'd gladly believe that this last remark doesn't apply equally to all juries, especially in the Seine Department.

There is no need to repeat here his account, which the newspapers have printed.

I note this odd aspect from the cross-examination: immediately after the burglary at N——, Bouboule met a worker whom he knew along the road at midnight, while returning to D——. What strange urge made him stop, when it would have been so simple to continue along, to ask him for a cigarette (perhaps he felt that this would seem more *natural* to the other man), and after a few minutes of conversation, suddenly struck by fear, to tell the other man: "Whatever you do, don't say that you met me tonight"?

The jurors voted to convict on all charges, and the court sentenced Prosper to life at hard labor.

Chapter 5

Another indecent assault, the fourth. This time the victim is under six years of age, the daughter of the defendant.

In this case, as in the others, I'd like to know what role opportunity plays. Would the crime have been committed had the defendant had any choice? And should we see preference in it, or just greater ease along with the deceptive promise of impunity?

Germain R—— defiled his daughter while his wife was in the hospital to give birth to another child.

He is small, ugly, of dismal appearance; his face is brutish. He wears a thick purple muffler over a yellowish black cotton jacket. He obstinately denies the charges, with a stupid, stubborn look. The testimony gathered about him is negative. "He thinks more about himself than about his family."

President: "Was he often drunk?"

Witness: "Every day, for the most part."

And another witness: "He gets drunk and lets his kids die of hunger."

Father, mother, and the two little ones, aged six and three all sleep on loose straw in a single room without a bed. It is claimed that he had already tried to lay hands on the girl before. Once he made her get into a sleeping bag with him. But he usually slept in a sleeping bag, and because this happened in wintertime, he could say that it was in order to warm up. We don't know. The little girl couldn't, or wouldn't, say anything. She was stood on a chair, to get her closer to the president's ear, and wept quietly, shaken by an occasional loud sob. No words could be drawn from her. It was as if she were afraid of being punished too. (She had been put in care. A man in livery with fat copper buttons brought her and then sat waiting on one of the witness benches.)

Then Madame R——, the defendant's wife, appeared. She wouldn't have been too ugly if her face hadn't been so terribly weather-beaten. She looked like a charwoman, wearing a short shawl of black wool over a blue apron. Her hair was pulled back and slicked down.

President: "What did you do to obviate this disadvantageous deed?"
Witness: ???

More than once the president asked a question in terms that were totally unintelligible to the witness or the accused. Such was the case now.

We proceeded to the cross-examination of the lone witness, the woman next door.

President: "In fact you saw nothing!"
Witness: "It's just that I came in either too early or too late."

Since after all we are uncertain what to believe, if we convict R——, it would be on presumptions (as often happens) and not so much for the alleged act, quite doubtful, but rather for his general behavior and to free his family from him.

❦ ❦ ❦

For the last case of the day, I was jury foreman again.

Joseph Galmier, aged twenty, son of Anaïs Albertine (What names they have! Last Saturday the poor woman X—— in the Z—— case, in which I found nothing unusual to relate, answered to the name of Adélaïde-Héloïse! Could it be poetic feeling that moves impoverished people to name their children so oddly?), is accused of committing two thefts, with aggravating circumstance. The deeds were done at night, in an inhabited house, by breaking and entering, and with accomplices.

Galmier is a day laborer at Le Havre. His face is not at all ugly but plain and ruddy. His nose is a bit too pointy, and with his hair brushed over his forehead and budding mustache, he looks like a Norman soldier by Cormon.[11] Well built and rather elegantly made, he wears a faded jacket over a sweater.

On a previous occasion he had been sentenced to six months' imprisonment.

Arrested at night in possession of a burglar's jimmy, he was in the company of prowlers equipped with passkeys.

He had made a complete confession in a letter to the district attorney but now said that a habitual criminal had forced him to write it. And he denied everything.

President: "Which habitual criminal?"

Defendant: "I don't dare mention his name. He threatened to take care of me when he gets out if I talk."

The president remained skeptical.

I am transcribing my notes as they are. It's possible that not all of them apply to this particular case.

The defendant, who spoke as quickly as possible, out of real fear that the president might cut him off (which he indeed did constantly), was no longer coherent as a result, and he knew it . . . an unfortunate man trying to save his own life.

Does an innocent man sound more eloquent and less disturbed than a guilty one? Nonsense! As soon as he feels that he isn't *believed,* he might be even more disturbed since he is less guilty. He'll overdo his statements, his protests will seem more and more disagreeable, and he will be out of his depth.

The police inspector's *doglike* aspect during his testimony, his arro-

11. Tr. note: Fernand Cormon (1845–1924; born Fernand-Anne Piestre) a French painter who taught Matisse, Toulouse-Lautrec, and van Gogh, was noted for scenes of local color and prehistory.

gant tone. The accused's immediately taking on the aspect of *prey*. The art of making him look guilty.

The unfortunate man who realizes, but only when he is undertaking it, that his defense is insufficient. His clumsy effort to strengthen it.

The criminal's imprudence and the kind of giddiness that leads him immediately to spend the sum he just stole. Galmier bought an overcoat, a suit, shirts, suspenders, handkerchiefs, ties, and so on. He gave a one-franc tip to the delivery man who brought him the package (he lived next door to the shop).

Professional criminals' joy when they meet a *novice*, undecided and a little foolish, who will agree to confess to their crime (they promise to pay for his lawyer).

The simplest version is always the likeliest to win acceptance. It's also the one with the least chance of being true.

☘ ☘ ☘

The next case brought five people before us. It should have been six, but one had escaped. The eldest is only twenty-two years old. It's a gang of pilferers accused of eight thefts. They've confessed to everything.

Janvier was caught first. The youngest, he refused to name his accomplices. Homeless for the previous eight days, he slept with another member of the same gang. Last February 12 he swiped a sausage from a window display, for which he was given a suspended sentence of fifteen days.

Janvier smiles easily, nicely. It's hard for him not to smile, he's so good-humored. He doesn't joke, but one senses a memory of the fun of theft still quivering in his replies, of thieving outings when they ventured out together. They played at stealing and pilfering. This joy would soon receive a severe cudgeling.

Can anyone ever recover from a prison sentence? Perhaps one recovers *all by oneself*?

"He can be saved now. Imprison him as a criminal, and I assure you that he will be lost."[12]

Chapter 6

A number of jurors got themselves excused. Therefore my name was often pulled from the ballot box, and for the ninth time I sat on a jury. In the jury room the others insisted that I be foreman, which Monsieur X—— entreated me to do in his place. It seems that he has the right to do so. As the only *intellectual,* more or less, among them, I feared hostility, despite the great effort I made to prevent it. Thus I was quite touched by this sign of esteem. It is true enough that during some of the preceding cases, the foreman turned out to be disturbingly inept, and his misunderstandings, hesitations, and clumsiness made deliberation and voting irritatingly slow.

The case offered no great interest in itself. It came to us from criminal court, where it actually belonged but which had declared itself unqualified to decide it.

At one o'clock in the morning Monsieur Granville, a day laborer in Rouen, was attacked on the rue de Barbot by a marauder who stole the two hundred-sou coins he had in his pocket. The victim stated that he would be unable to recognize his aggressor, but his shouts made Madame Ridel put her nose to the window. She claimed to recognize him as a certain Monsieur Valentin, a day laborer, who was summoned to appear before us.

Valentin desperately denied it and claimed to have been asleep at home all night. First off, how could Madame Ridel have recognized him? It was a moonless night, and the street was very dimly lit.

Whereupon Madame Ridel protested that the attack took place right by a gaslight.

We questioned the policeman who helped investigate the case. Among other witnesses we questioned, one located the gaslight at five

---

12. The words John Galsworthy gave to the defense lawyer in his play *Justice.* [Tr. note: Here Gide quotes, in English, a speech from the 1910 play by Galsworthy (1845–1924), which shows how a young man who commits a minor crime is destroyed by the British penal system.]

meters away and another, at twenty-five meters. A last one went so far as to claim that there was no gaslight at all on this part of the street.

But Valentin had a wicked past and a deplorable reputation, and although the deputy district attorney, who led the prosecution, didn't manage to prove that Valentin was guilty, the defense attorney didn't manage to persuade us that he was innocent. Undecided, what would the jury do? They would vote him guilty, yet with extenuating circumstances, to lessen the jury's responsibility. How many times (even in the Dreyfus case) have "extenuating circumstances" meant nothing more than a jury's total bafflement! As soon as there is even slight indecision, a juror is inclined to vote that way, and even more so if the crime is a serious one. This means yes, the crime is very serious, but we're not really sure that this is the man who committed it. Still, some punishment is necessary, so just in case, let's punish the man, since he's the one offered to us as a victim. But since we're not sure, let's at any rate not punish him too much.

In many cases that I've been called on to decide, I was troubled, as were all the jurors who ruled with me, by the great difficulty of imagining the scene of the crime, the *site* of the action, based only on witnesses' testimony and the defendant's cross-examination. In certain cases this is of the highest importance. For example, here it was a matter of knowing how far from a gaslight an attack had occurred. Could a given witness, situated at a given spot, have recognized the attacker? Was he sufficiently illuminated for this? We know the exact place of the attack. About the distance between the attacker and the gaslight, *all* the witnesses differ. One says five meters; another, twenty-five. However, it would have been easy for the police to note down a *map* of the place, so that each juror could be given a copy at the start of the session. I think that in many cases, this map could have been of real use.

On the same day, a third case. During a dispute with X——, Conrad stabbed her several times, causing her death.

I noted down, during this final part of the session, which was otherwise uninteresting:

How rarely a case presents itself simply and *in order*.

How often it happens that the indictment's simplified representation of the facts is artificial.

How easily it occurs that a defendant gets tangled up in a secondary statement of whose seriousness he is at first unaware.

"So, *mad with rage . . .* ," says Conrad in his explanation (referring to his stabbing his mistress just as she was about to kill him).

The president immediately interrupts him:

"You hear that, gentlemen of the jury, *mad with rage.*"

And the district attorney triumphantly seizes on the unfortunate phrase, which the accused now cannot take back, whereas it's clear that this is just an oratorical expression that Conrad, who is very mindful of eloquence, threw in purely for the sound of it.

Chapter 7

Tuesday

Another indecent assault, the last we will be required to judge. This one was particularly arduous, for the defendant, a young day laborer from Maromme,[13] infected the victim with gonorrhea. The worst information was conveyed about him. An insolent drunkard and slapdash worker, he had already once tried to lure a little girl, aged ten, into the woods by offering her pocket change and candy.

The girl who appeared as a witness before us was only six-and-a-half years old. He got her into his room by offering her "a small snuff box."

She was obliged to repeat in detail for us what she said before at the preliminary investigation and what the guilty man admitted, verified by a doctor. They seemed to be most insistent that the little girl remember. In fact, she had not exactly been raped. It seems that the defendant took certain precautions for her sake, perhaps hoping she would thereby not be infected, thanks to which he benefited from extenuating circumstances.

13. Tr. note: Maromme is a small city in Normandy, in the region of Rouen.

❦ ❦ ❦

The Charles case, which we judged next, had made a certain echo in the press. The room was full, for it was a "sensational" case with a highly excited audience. From bench to bench they repeated the number of times the victim had been stabbed—the doctor counted no fewer than 110 wounds!

The victim was Charles's mistress. Juliette R—— was only seventeen years old when he met her for the first time, three years before. She was living with a lover, whom Charles immediately replaced, abandoning a wife and children after eleven years of marriage. Charles was thirty-four years old, a coachman who has been through several jobs, but the information gathered about him from various employers is positive. Nor did his wife have any complaints about him, although he sometimes caused "scenes." After he moved in with the young woman, Madame Charles tried several times to bring him home, to take him back, but nothing worked. The preliminary investigation stated that he had the girl "under his skin, as the expression goes." At that time he lived with Juliette R—— at the Place de M——, in a house owned by Madame Gilet, who sometimes heard them arguing.

"That's true. Juliette objected to my sending part of my salary to my children, but I never threatened her."

And Madame Gilet admitted that their quarrels were infrequent and brief.

Charles has a deep voice, and his appearance is pleasant. He is large, strong, and well-built, yet without being in any way a fop or conceited person. Just by looking at him, one can tell that he's a coachman and not a cab man—a family coachman.

He doesn't defend himself or even excuse himself. One feels he is anxious to present the facts such as they occurred, without seeking to influence the jury in his favor. Why is the president trying to make him give himself away and contradict himself? Doubtless from professional habit, as a former examining magistrate.

"You have varied just a bit," he told him, "in your account of the motives of the crime."

It's just that Charles cannot explain very well to himself how or why he killed her. He loved the woman madly and *needed* her. On the evening of March 12, the day before the crime, they ate a late supper together.

"After supper I went to bed with her as usual, but she refused to give herself. That's how it started."

"You argued with her then?"

"Because of that, yes."

"That's the motive you give for the crime. Yet at first you gave another explanation."

The defendant did not object, making a gesture that seems to say, it's possible.

"The rest of the night was quiet?"

"Yes, sir."

"You also said that you were jealous. Indeed, that was the explanation that you gave at first. Did you know if she had a lover?"

"She didn't have one."

"Yet she was sad; at the Abeilles store where she worked, they said she was anxious, that she was afraid of you. One day she took away your razor. Was she worried you might use it on her?"

"I was ill at the time. She was told to take it away from me so I wouldn't use it to harm myself."

"Let's get to March 13."

"We said hello in the morning, and I went down to get the newspaper."

"You didn't drink anything?"

"The previous night, before supper, I had two cups of coffee at B——, but that morning I hadn't had anything. Coming back to her, I asked her once again. She refused again. Since she still didn't want it, I lost my head. I took a knife from the table near me and stabbed her in the neck. *The knife stuck in my hand.*"

"She was still in bed?"

"For the first stab, yes."

"Then she tried to escape, jumping out of bed. You threw yourself on her, and she fell down."

"Yes, finally I found her on the floor."

"Finally? Not so fast! We're still at the beginning. She fell on the floor, as we were saying. That's when you continued to stab her like a mad-man, covering her neck, face, and wrists with knife wounds."

"I only remember the first stab."

"That's too easy. You stabbed her more than one hundred times. According to one witness's statement, you held her on the floor with one hand, and with the other you stabbed her everywhere."

"When I came to, Juliette was dead. I was leaning over her, and there was blood everywhere. I hadn't seen Madame Gilet come in."

"Hearing the unfortunate woman's screams, she had come to help. She saw you stab her with such violence and speed that she said, using a striking image, that it resembled the stamping of letters at the post office. Do you hear, gentlemen of the jury, the stamping of letters at the post office!"

Thereupon the president added mime to his words, pounding his hollow desk heavily to make a thunderous sound that sent an unseemly laugh rippling through the court. Surely that's not what it sounded like.

"Your mistress screamed: 'Ah! Ma'am, save me! He has a knife!' Then you pushed Madame Gilet away, bloodying her with your touch. 'Get out of here. This doesn't concern you,' you told her. Then, going back to stab the unfortunate woman one last time, you severed her caryatid [*sic*]."[14] (Soon thereafter Madame Gilet would say that the last stab wound was "aimed at the forehead.") "What have you to say?"

"I don't remember any of that."

"Yet when the policemen came, called by Madame Gilet, they were amazed at your self-possession. You didn't even look upset, it seems. The knife was on the table. You let yourself be arrested."

"I was dazed with horror."

"Not at all! You said calmly, 'Tell my wife,' and when the police were going to take you away, you asked for permission to wash your hands before going into the street."

"I do recall having provided my wife's address, so that she could be notified."

"After that, didn't you want to hang yourself?"

"Never."

14. Tr. note: The judge has confused *carotide,* which means "carotid artery," with *cariatide,* a type of sculpture used as an architectural ornament.

"That was suspected. We found in the room an eyebolt strong enough to support a heavy weight, and we also found a thin strap. Didn't you then speak of a wish for suicide?"

"I never said that."

"No matter. When all is said and done, you've admitted the facts, and you give this explanation for your crime, that Juliette refused to give herself to you."

"That morning, I saw something frightful happening before my eyes."

"At any rate, she is dead, poor young woman! If she didn't want you anymore, all you had to do was go back to your wife and children. Why kill her?"

"I wasn't trying to kill her." (An indignant murmur went through the courtroom.)

"Come now! Stabbing her one hundred times!"

Most of the jurors agreed with the president that someone is more intent on killing when he stabs one hundred times than when he stabs just once. Yet the medical examination of the victim informed us that the 110 wounds located on the face, neck, upper thorax, and hands (the majority were on the neck) were methodically placed, and all were small and shallow. (In Russia this surely would have been seen as a "ritual crime.") A single wound had hit the carotid and caused the lethal bleeding.

As I wasn't on the jury, I could not ask whether the fact that none of the wounds was deep was due to the shape and size of the weapon. It did not seem so; the doctor would say soon after that Charles had stabbed "in a trembling manner, with little penetration, as if he only wanted to mutilate."

His fingers were injured, certainly caused by the victim's trying to protect herself.

The widow Augustine Gilet, landlady, called to testify, gave her deposition in a monotonous voice:

"Charles and the young woman Juliette lived in my house. I had no complaints about them. On the morning of March 13 I heard screaming and went to their room. She was on the floor, and I saw him hitting her.

I grabbed his arm to hold him back. He turned around and said, 'Get out of here.' Juliette wasn't dead; when she saw me trying to hold him back, she told me, 'Ah! Be careful, he has a knife!' Then he stabbed her again, and when he turned the knife in the wound, it went, 'crrack!'" (A shudder of horror and a murmur in the crowd. Even the jurors were very stirred by Madame Gilet's story, particularly the last detail. After a request from the defense attorney, however, Doctor X—— would tell us shortly: "None of the injuries suggest that the knife was turned in a wound.")

"It's as if the knife had trouble penetrating. I was stunned. He stabbed quickly, the way letters are stamped. He stabbed her maybe twenty-five times while I was there. When I tried to stop him and he turned around, he got blood on me. I was in my dressing gown, and later I found I was covered in blood. I was so scared, I didn't notice the state the room was in. Only later did I see that the bed was drenched with blood. The night before, I hadn't heard any noise. No one came to their room. Juliette was quiet and worked regularly. We had no problems with her. With him either. They behaved well. I never saw him drunk."

"Is that all you can say about him?"

"Last summer, after he took a fall, he was ailing for a long while. My first idea when I saw him strike Juliette was that he had gone mad. He seemed to love her a lot. Only when Juliette said, 'He has a knife' did I realize he was armed. Until that moment, I thought he was hitting her with his fist."

Charles: "I didn't see Madame Gilet; I had a feeling she was there, that's all."

Madame Gilet: "After a bloodbath like that, I can understand that he took leave of his senses. The last stab must have been aimed at the forehead. But it was dark, around 5:45, and I could barely see. Before this, nothing in Charles's behavior could have predicted this tragedy. When they argued, they made it up, with very little fighting."

Mademoiselle Gilet, called in turn, would say:

"Sometimes they squabbled, but five minutes later they would be kissing again."

After the testimony from the landlady and her daughter, we heard from the police.

The police station chief M—— stated, "When we wanted to take the accused to the station, he told us, 'At least give me time to wash my hands.' He did not appear to be either drunk or insane. He was rather calm."

And Monsieur V——, the police superintendent: "I saw Charles at headquarters. He was a little edgy, but not drunk. He told me, after some hesitation: 'I killed her because she cost me too much. What's more, I was going to throw myself into the river when I was arrested.'"

President: "Well then! You see, Charles, your first explanation of this crime's motive isn't the same as the one you've given us today. Go ahead, speak."

Defendant: "What do you want me to say? I told you the truth."

Monsieur V——: "I had a feeling that he wasn't telling it then and was hiding the motive for the crime. Indeed, he gave different reasons today. It all seemed very strange. I took him by the hands, and lifted up his eyelids, but he wasn't drunk or insane."

Madame Charles came to the witness box to testify that for ten years, or until he met the young woman Juliette, she had nothing for which to reproach her husband.

Doctor X—— is summoned to speak about Charles. He presents him as, at first, a healthy and sound boy, with no hereditary defects. But he had six fingers on one hand, was prone to dizziness and bouts of amnesia, and had trouble orienting himself. He made errors in pronunciation (I confess that I hadn't noticed them) and was afraid of falling down in the street. The doctor also spoke of instability of judgment, indecision, and absence of will (wasn't this what allowed for that sudden transformation of unsatisfied desire into energy?) and finally concluded by saying that, without his being in a state of dementia, such as it is described in article 64 of the penal code, "a psychiatric and biological examination, as well as the specially impulsive nature of his crime, indicates a mental anomaly that diminishes his responsibility."

"As he stated a few moments ago, his act was done without the idea of killing being quite specified in his mind. The proof of this lies in the distribution of stab wounds, as I've described."

Why didn't the defense attorney go further and say that not only had

Charles not *wanted* to kill but that he dimly tried, while mutilating his victim, not to kill her and that, doubtless so as not to kill her, *he had grabbed the knife just next to the blade,* which is the only way that the stabbing could have been so intense yet cause such shallow wounds and which left Charles with cuts on his fingers (the doctor's report)? Wasn't that also the reason Madame Gilet didn't see the knife and thought he was hitting her with his fist?

None of that was said by Monsieur R——, the accused's defense counsel. He relied on the doctors' report to ask the jurors not to go further than the experts and admit extenuating circumstances for the defendant.

I have dwelled at length on this case, for it made obvious the appalling incompetence of jurors. As emerged unmistakably from the preliminary investigation, testimony, and medical reports, the idea of killing was not clearly established in Charles's brain. In any event, this was no professional criminal, and perhaps more a sadist than a murderer. If ever a crime could be called one of passion . . .

After a half-hour of deliberation, the jurors could be seen returning into the room, flushed and wild-eyed as if scalded, each furious with the others and with himself. They brought back a guilty verdict on the sole count of murder put by the court. As for extenuating circumstances, *asked for even by the prosecution*—although little given to clemency—they rejected them.

As a result Charles was sentenced to life imprisonment at hard labor.

Heinous applause broke out in the room. There were shouts of "Bravo! Bravo!" from the crowd, in a frenzy. But Charles's wife, who had remained in the room, rose up, seized by acute anguish, shouting, "It's too much! Ah, it's too much!" and fainted. She was helped out.

Immediately after the session, the jurors, disturbed by the results of their vote (had they not realized that not to vote yes on extenuating circumstances was the same as voting no?), regrouped and, rushing to another extreme, unanimously signed a petition for reprieve.

Had Madame Gilet not said that the knife turning in the wound went "crrack!" they would doubtless have simply voted for extenuating circumstances right away.

It might partially explain the jurors' panic if I state that the day before, a lead article appeared in the *Journal de Rouen,* "Jurors and the Law of Suspended Sentences" (issue of May 17, 1912), that I saw passed from hand to hand, so that all my colleagues, or almost all of them, had read it. The article spoke out against leniency, taking as its pretext a case that had just been judged in Paris, where the jury's verdict had forced the court to acquit three young brigands. The text ran as follows:

> Parisian juries have never given a greater sign of weakness than in the case where, to widespread amazement, they acquitted three young burglars proven guilty of having tried to rob a home....
>
> The outrageous and absurd leniency in this particular case may perhaps be explained by the plaintiff's extraordinary attitude, for he requested that his aggressors be acquitted and even, it appears, demonstrated an intention to adopt one of them....[15] But we need hardly point out that the jurors, who must have steady minds and some experience of the world, could not have fallen prey to such inane sentimentality (*that "inane" isn't very Christian, Monsieur Journalist*) and, as a result, have betrayed their duty by refusing to convict avowed criminals, who have no redeeming qualities.
>
> This strange verdict, which the press has universally condemned....
>
> In our day, when crime is on the increase, when the audacity and ferocity of criminals surpass all known limits (*O Flaubert!*),[16] when even youngsters enter boldly onto the paths of evil ...

Who can measure the power of persuasion—or intimidation—of a printed page on minds not well equipped for criticism and for the most part conscientious, so willing to do the right thing?

A few days ago one of the jurors confided, "The president told me that up to now we have judged very well." This passing grade from the president went from mouth to mouth, and each juror lit up when he repeated it. They would shortly be cast down again.

15. How interesting it would be to know the result of this unusual experiment!

16. Tr. note: Gide's ironic interjection invokes Gustave Flaubert (1821–80), whose fascination with clichés was expressed in his posthumously published *Dictionnaire des idées reçues* (Dictionary of received ideas; 1913), which has been called a "surreal, aphoristic encyclopedia of human stupidity."

Chapter 8

At first considered a simple misdemeanor, the case we were to judge that day had already been before Le Havre's criminal court. One of the two defendants, protesting his two-year sentence, had filed an appeal. He was Yves Cordier, a shoemaker, summoned along with his accomplices, C. Lepic and Henri Goret, and two young women, Mélanie and Gabrielle. All five were accused of having lured the sailor Braz to an isolated place, after getting him drunk, in order to "beat him up" and steal his money. The sailor, who was back on duty, could not answer the summons, nor could he testify when the case went to criminal court. He lodged his complaint immediately after the attack. Once he recovered his money, he withdrew the complaint a few days later and shipped out again. The case proceeded, but only in spite of him.

Cordier was a large fellow, eighteen years old, a bit fat, blond, and blue-eyed, with an open face that one could easily imagine smiling. He looked like a sailor, although he still wore a reddish-brown prison tunic. He wept continuously, sometimes mopping his face with a checked handkerchief that he rolled into a ball with his right hand. His left hand was wrapped in cloth.

Lepic was a day laborer from Le Havre. The civil register said he was twenty-five years old, and he looked, as they say, like a nasty customer. He had high cheekbones, an enormous mustache, and a pointy nose. It was no surprise to learn that he had already been sentenced seven times for theft. He held a little cap in his hands, which were frightfully gnarled and, one might say, badly designed. He wore no undershirt, or at least none that showed.

Next to him Henri Goret looked lost. This young man of apparent good social standing didn't seem to be from the same class as the rest; he wore an undershirt and even a stand-up collar, and his thin tie had a stiff knot. His face, with its nascent mustache, would have been almost pretty had it not been moronic and debased. His voice was weak, hollow, and husky; he didn't know what to do with his fat, swollen hands. Goret's father ran a pub and a cheap hotel near the docks. Henri Goret was under twenty years old. He had married a whore who got herself thrown into prison soon after the wedding, but no matter! Henri made a good impression. Certainly the decorum, and I was going to say the distinction, of his garb predisposed the jurors in his favor, showing up the commonness and penury of the two others.

Let's proceed to the account of the "violent scenes in which these individuals are implicated," as the *Journal de Rouen* (May 16) wrote:

On the evening of October 4, 1911, Cordier met Lepic. Doubtless the latter quickly understood the kind of easy-going, good-natured man with whom he was dealing. They went to the Folies together, and when the show ended, they started to roam the streets. They met two sailors, Braz and Crochu. Crochu was dead drunk, difficult to pull along; Braz called to the two others and asked if they knew a room where they could put the drunk to bed. All three took Crochu to the rue de la Girafe, to Lestocard's place. They left him there, and Braz, thankful for Lepic and Cordier's help, offered to buy them a drink.

They emerged from Lestocard's arm-in-arm and spent some time together. At the Place du Vieux-Marché, they met two women, the prostitutes Gabrielle and Mélanie, who joined them. By then it was two o'clock in the morning. At the Place Gambetta Cordier offered to buy a round of drinks. Then they went back to Place du Vieux-Marché; Braz paid for another round at the café Fortin. At this time young Goret joined them. He happened to be in the café, near the counter, but he himself wasn't drunk. When the others went out, he left too. I assume that Braz, who was already drunk, didn't pay much attention to him.

By then it was nearly 4 A.M., and Braz was ready to go to bed, but the others pulled him along. All six wandered around at random, finally reaching rue Casimir-Delavigne. Braz was worn out and wanted to be left alone: "Now it's time to go to bed." But Lepic didn't see it that way, trying to lure him outside the city:

"Come on along! I've got a garden up there, near the Fort de Tourneville. We'll pick roses. I'll give you a bouquet that you'll remember for a long time" (the prostitute Gabrielle's testimony).

In vain did Gabrielle pull the sailor by the sleeve, trying to hold him back, but he was no longer in a condition to hear anything or listen to reason. They all started off and began to ascend the long hillside.

One of the prostitutes leaned toward the other: "You don't think this is going to end in trouble? For sure they're going to do him in."

"No," the other replied, "there are always some soldiers near the fort."

Braz was between Lepic and "the one with his hand in a sling" (testimony of Braz). This "hand in a sling" made a big impression on him. The prostitutes followed, with Goret some distance behind.

At five o'clock, or just before dawn (October 5), they walked down into the fort's trench, on who knows what pretext, while the two prostitutes stayed above.

What happened next is difficult to say with any certainty. The sailor was no longer there to tell. Moreover, at the moment of the attack, he was drunk and probably could only vaguely realize the way he was being attacked and the individual role of each assailant. Our only explanation, therefore, was the testimony of the other persons involved. Now, all the defendants claimed to be innocent, or at least each tried to limit his share of responsibility as far as possible. (Lepic, more categorically, denied even having been along with them: they were mistaken; it wasn't him.)

We moved on to Cordier's cross-examination.

No doubt he was a wicked fellow, having already been convicted three times for theft. The first time he was only fourteen years old, and he was returned to his parents. He did it again and once again was sent back to his family, but the third time he was sent to a disciplinary colony. He was so horrified by the conditions there that he ran away, going back to his mother. Madame Cordier was a sailor's widow who ran a laundry, where she employed several female workers. Yves Cordier was the youngest of five children. One of the younger brothers was in the army. The rest were stable and married, with respectable careers, and the whole family was considered honorable. The youngest one, who concerns us, seemed particularly well-loved, not only by his mother and brothers, but also by the neighbors. His employers spoke highly of him, and one letter read out in court praised his "conduct and probity" and asked to rehire him. Cordier had already returned to work in this office two days after being let out of prison for the first time.[17]

17. I'm noting only the information here that was given to us by the court, not what I independently gathered later on.

Cordier's testimony agrees in all details with that of the two young women. According to their account, Goret suddenly leapt at the sailor's neck from behind and rolled on the ground with him. While Lepic gagged him, Goret searched him and passed the money found in his pockets to Cordier. Almost immediately Cordier passed the money back to Lepic. Goret gave the sailor two last kicks in the neck, and they left.

Each went in his own direction, but they made a date to meet up a bit later at Goret's room on the rue du Petit-Croissant to divide up the money.

That's where the police, immediately called by the sailor, arrested them.

The president rushed through the cross-examination of the two prostitutes. It was clear that he saw the witnesses, "of dubious morality," as untrustworthy, which was only natural. Unfortunately, they were the only ones who could have enlightened us. Gabrielle fielded one question after another, so quickly that she had no time to finish her replies, and sensing that the president didn't trust her, she became flustered. She answered yes or no, barely getting a monosyllable in edgewise. She wanted to say (at least I thinks so) that Cordier took no part in the attack and only received the money that the others passed on to him. That wasn't so easy to do! Obviously all this had already been explained in the preliminary investigation. For the judge studying the case, the cross-examination couldn't and *shouldn't* add anything new, but for the juror, everything is new. He is trying to develop an opinion, worrying and wondering whether the judgment might be reached too quickly, like the president's opinion of it.

President: "Did Cordier put his hand over the victim's mouth?"

The prostitute Gabrielle: "No, Your Honor."

President: "Then he's the one who hit him?"

The prostitute Gabrielle: "No, Your Honor."

President: "So, one hit him, another gagged him, and a third searched him. Braz says that Cordier hit him, but you say that Cordier only frisked him. No doubt there was some confusion in the struggle and therefore in the testimonies as well. It clearly emerges from all this that the three defendants were equally involved and responsible. Mademoiselle Gabrielle, you may step down."

The prostitute Gabrielle was the last witness, and we move on to the counsels' speeches. Then the president, according to custom, turns toward the man "with his hand in a sling":

"You haven't anything to add to the witness's report?"

Cordier, who felt that everything was over, sobbed:

"Your Honor, I tol' the truth. I didn't touch him." Then, with a pathetic outburst that made the worst impression: "I swear it on my father's grave . . ."

President: "My boy, leave your father out of it."

Cordier, continuing: ". . . not even with the tip of my finger."

No exculpatory witnesses had been heard for Cordier or any of the others. The letter from one of Cordier's employers was read aloud, but why didn't his mother testify? Because Yves Cordier didn't want her to be summoned and even refused to furnish her address.

President: "Why didn't you want to provide your mother's address?"

Cordier made no reply.

President: "So you refuse to tell us why you didn't want to provide your mother's address?"

Alas, Your Honor, is it really so difficult to understand, or can't you allow that Cordier might have wanted to spare his mother the shame? If you could have seen the poor woman, as I did later,[18] doubtless you would no longer be astonished.

I was horrified and dismayed to feel that the cross-examination was about to end and that Cordier's individual case would remain so incompletely and so badly exposed. For I knew almost nothing about him, but already it seemed to me that the boy had nothing ferocious about him, nothing of a bandit. It even seemed possible that he joined the sailor because he was moved by a vague sympathy. Could I not come up with some question, since as a juror I have the right to ask them, to enlighten the court and myself as well—for perhaps I'm wrong and perhaps Yves

18. "I certainly won't refuse to give you my mother's address," Cordier wrote to me shortly afterward from prison, "since I only refused to give it to the judge so that she wouldn't come to the courthouse."

Cordier might not in fact deserve pity? Once the lawyers' speeches began, I'd no longer have the right to add questions. Only a moment remained, and Cordier's lawyer was already getting up. In a choked voice, my heart beating, I *read* the following, which I had just written down, fearing that otherwise I might not find the words and finish my sentence:

"Your Honor, could we know what sum was taken from the victim and how it was shared proportionally among the defendants?"

The president proceeded to a short cross-examination, and we learned that ninety-two francs had been taken from Braz. Of this sum, five francs was given to each of the two women to buy their silence. Cordier received ten francs, which he immediately gave back to the attackers, and the remaining seventy-two francs were evenly divided between Lepic and Goret.

Ah, if only it were possible for me to draw conclusions aloud, and from these numbers, to evaluate each individual's share of responsibility! Would Cordier's lawyer do it, at least? No, his defense speech was otherwise solid and skillful, but he could not behave as if his client did not already have a heavy police record. Nor could he alter the fact that shortly after his arrest—or more exactly, I believe, after the first preliminary investigation—Cordier wrote the most absurd, insane letter to the district attorney:

"I don't know Lepic or Goret," he wrote. "They weren't there. I did the job alone, with one of my friends from the port. I regret only one thing: not having finished off the sailor."

A letter obviously written under pressure from Lepic, the defense attorney would say, and doubtless as a result of his threats. (Lepic also tried to intimidate the two women and threatened them with his "Catalonian" knife.) Cordier was likely persuaded that as a minor he was at little risk, since he could not be given a heavy sentence.

Although the prosecution mentioned this letter, it did not place great stock in it. Sometimes, and even often, the district attorney receives this sort of "confession" from prison, which sometimes enlightens the court and sometimes distracts it. Sometimes such letters are written in the idleness of jail with no rhyme or reason, but no matter! In the jurors' minds, this letter had the most damaging effect. For myself, I had the greatest difficulty relating it to the little of Cordier's character (and lack of character) that was revealed in the hearing.

After the first defense speech, the court recessed and we went to dinner.

Two hours later, when we returned to the courthouse, Cordier's lawyer was *no longer there.* I wouldn't go so far as to say that the lawyers for the other two prisoners took advantage of that absence, but since the only way they could get their clients off was to accuse Cordier, the presence of Cordier's defender might have been useful. Instead, Cordier was at the mercy of the other two men's discretion.

That's not the only way that Cordier suffered by being tried first. No doubt the jurors would have been less intransigent had they first vented their severity on Lepic. By appearing last, Goret benefited from a reaction; moreover, his garb, behavior, and sly appearance favorably impressed the jury.

No sooner were we in the jury room than a tall, thin, white-haired "foreman" pulled from his pocket a paper on which he had written all the charges against Cordier and, most important, his previous convictions. In truth these would dominate and determine this latest verdict. That's how difficult it is for a juror not to consider a previous conviction as an indictment and to judge a defendant outside the shadow that a previous conviction casts on him.

In vain did another juror read aloud an extremely favorable letter from another of Cordier's employers—a letter that had not been added to the transcript and was given to him by I know not whom or what means while we were going to the jury room—which I thought was strictly forbidden.

"Bandits, the whole lot of them," another juror stated. "Got to get rid of them for society's sake."

That's what we did, as much as was possible. Cordier was sentenced to five years' imprisonment and ten years' exile. As I write these words, Goret has already been free for three months.

That night I couldn't sleep, as the anguish in my heart didn't lessen its grip for a moment. I thought of the story once told me in Le Havre

by a survivor of the *Bourgogne*:[19] He was in a lifeboat with I don't recall how many others. Some were rowing, while others used oars to rain
blows on the heads and hands of half-drowned people who clung to
the side of the boat, begging to be taken aboard. Others had their wrists
hacked at with small axes before being shoved underwater, for trying
to save them would have capsized the boat, which was already full in
any case.

Yes, the best thing is not to fall into the water. Afterward, if heaven
doesn't help you, it's damned hard to escape! That night I was ashamed
of the boat and of knowing myself to be safely inside it.

Before going back to bed, I wandered for a long time in the sad neigh-
borhood near the port, inhabited by sad people for whom prison seems
a natural residence—blackened by coal, drunk on bad wine, drunk
without joy, hideous. And in the sordid streets, small children prowled,
gaunt and unsmiling, ill-clothed, ill-nourished, unloved.

But Cordier is the son of a respectable family; he was given good
examples. If we lend him a helping hand, perhaps he might be saved.

The next morning I went to find his lawyer and offered the following draft of a petition (it contains a request not for a pardon but simply for a lesser sentence):

Whereas

the only testimony against the defendant Cordier is that of the victim,
Monsieur Braz, drunk at the time of his attack;

and whereas, moreover, Monsieur Braz, a sailor, has set off again on
his travels, unable to be reached by summons and therefore to testify at
the hearing;

and whereas, nevertheless, from his first testimony it transpires that he
was attacked from behind and could not see his attacker;

additionally,

whereas

Cordier's testimony concurs completely with that of the prostitutes
Gabrielle and Mélanie, the only witnesses to the attack, from which ac-

19. Tr. note: The wreck of the French ship *La Bourgogne*, on July 4, 1898, in which five hundred people were lost, was much discussed in the press. Gide also mentions this shipwreck
in his novel *The Counterfeiters*.

count it has emerged that Cordier in no way took part in the attack but merely received the victim's money, which the two attackers, Goret and Lepic, handed to him;

and whereas it emerges from the testimony that Goret, much less drunk than the others, not having participated in any of the previous "rounds," followed the group from a distance, without Braz's knowledge, up to the moment when he leapt upon him; that Lepic lured the sailor with a specific intention; and that Cordier, with a weak character, nearly incapable of resisting the lure, and what's more, completely drunk, apparently did nothing but follow along;

and whereas this is confirmed by the fact that when the money was divided, Goret and Lepic kept the major part, judging it sufficient to give him ten francs, just as they had given five francs to each of the two prostitutes, as the price for their silence;

and whereas

Cordier's statement, taken during the preliminary investigation, which the defense attorneys of the other defendants, and the district attorney, have made use of—"I'm the only one who did the job with another friend; neither Lepic nor Goret were there; I only regret one thing, not having finished him off"—is clearly inspired by a fear of Lepic, a dangerous habitual criminal—who similarly tried to intimidate the two women—and therefore there is no reason to heed this statement;

and whereas

if Cordier was guilty (at least to the extent that has been claimed), it is totally unlikely that he would have sought to have his case transferred to another jurisdiction, as he did when the Le Havre criminal court sentenced him to two years' imprisonment.

. . . .

The lawyer helpfully showed me the formal changes he thought should be made to it, stressing the pathologist's report stating that Cordier is "of below average intelligence, expressing himself with a certain difficulty, and his memory sometimes fails him," resulting in diminished responsibility. Then he showed me the steps to get it signed and approved by the district attorney and to send it to the proper authorities.

A sort of timidity, and a fear, too, of obtaining nothing by asking for too much, a sense of justice—for after all, I couldn't consider Cordier to be innocent—kept me from asking for a simple pardon. I realized later that it wouldn't have been any more difficult to obtain. Indeed, several of the jurors had given this case some thought; they had made up their minds during the night; they were ready to approve my petition, and I had no problem collecting signatures from eight of them. One of the others, an enormous red-faced farmer, bursting with health, joy, and ignorance, overhearing us speak of a prisoner's illness and that lack of care would harm his condition, boomed out: "If he croaks, so much the better for society. What's the use of curing him? Should tell him what the doctor told that other guy who wanted his rotted finger cut off—'Don't bother, my boy! It'll fall off on its own.'"

I should add that this jest drew laughter from only a few people.

The two others who refused to sign gave as a reason that they had voted in accordance with their consciences and that we'd have far too much to do if we had to reexamine each case that was tried.

Certainly. All the same, I would like to have seen the records for Cordier's last two sentencings. If he was judged then as we judged him yesterday![20]

20. As soon as I had a day free, I went to Le Havre and visited the accused's mother. I had some difficulty in finding her, for the poor woman had been forced to change her address to flee her neighbors' attention and insulting remarks. Once she realized why I had come, she led me to a separate little room where the female workers she employed couldn't hear us.

She sobbed and could barely speak; one of her daughters accompanied her, finishing her mother's stories:

"Ah, sir," the mother told me, "it was a great misfortune for us when my other son (the younger one) joined the military. He used to give good advice, which Yves always obeyed. When he escaped from the colony, he didn't dare live at home, for fear that he might be recaptured. That's when he started to see terrible people, when he was homeless, people who led him on and ruined him."

All the information that I subsequently gathered about Yves Cordier—from his mother and sister, from his most recent employer, and from his brother, whom I went to see at the military base—entirely confirmed the opinion that I began to form:

Yves Cordier was weak minded, lacked judgment, and was deplorably easy to lead astray. They all called him kindly to a fault, which also means lacking any resistance. His desire to oblige others became a form of mania, or idiocy. To help a friend "who was in need," Yves Cordier stole an old pair of shoes, his first theft.

While he was in the prison colony, his mother obtained permission to bring him sweets. The guard told her, "If you're bringing that for him, ma'am, it isn't worth it; he gives everything away to others and will keep nothing for himself."

In the colony he took a friend's advice and had the back of his left hand tattooed. Soon afterward another friend convinced him that a tattoo could work against him in life, so Yves, obeying this new advice, applied a plaster made of salt and vitriol over the tattoo that ate away the skin down to the bone (that's why, on the day of the crime, he had his hand in a sling).

"The boy just needed to be controlled," the shoemaker who employed him told me, speaking of him with great emotion and eagerly asking to rehire him.

Some time later my petition was granted, and Cordier's sentence was reduced to three years' imprisonment.

But alas, after prison he will go to an African regiment, and six years later, who will he be? *What* will he be?

Chapter 9

The most "important" case was left for last. The one that occupied us on the last day threatened to go on for so long that we were summoned at nine o'clock that morning. The session would continue until after ten o'clock that night, interrupted twice for mealtimes. At issue were a number of thefts, committed at the Sotteville freight depot, of merchandise entrusted to the federal railway company.

Since new directors first took over this company, numerous claims have been filed against them, and from all sides there are complaints of innumerable thefts, some of them quite serious.

A loud sigh of relief was heard from the press and public when it was learned that a large gang of thieves and receivers of stolen goods had been nabbed. We were offered no fewer than sixteen to be judged; from the beginning of the session, rumor had it that we would have to respond to over one hundred counts.

Reading the bill of indictment caused us some astonishment. We expected something more or better; given the great sums involved in some of the misappropriations, of which the jurors reminded one another before the session began, the pilfering allegedly committed by these defendants seemed to us mere peccadilloes, and astonishment quickly changed to boredom, fatigue, and even, for some of the jurors, irritation and exasperation as the cross-examination proceeded.

An endless discussion began, attempting to determine whether three and a half bottles of Cointreau had been stolen by Madame X—— or purchased by her, as she maintained, from Madame B——, who, however, maintains that Madame X—— never bought any liqueurs from her. Also wanting to give evidence, Madame X—— carries in her arms a tiny crying baby.

X——, the defendant's husband, admits having appropriated "the remnants of a bottle of kirsch," but he never gave a pair of socks to Y——;

on the contrary, he received them from him. As for the carving knife and fork, it was Z—— who . . . , and so on.

X—— is a good worker and a father of four, earning one hundred sous per day, plus expenses. His testimony concurs with that of B——, who says he received mustard from N—— and coffee and tea from M——, all in derisory amounts. By contrast, he didn't receive anything from D—— or E——. He admitted having accompanied N—— when he swiped a mustard pot, but he himself took nothing. N—— makes no bones about admitting the theft of a mustard pot.

M—— is also a father of four, and he admits the appropriation of five kilos of rice and a few pieces of coal. It was he who gave B—— two kilos of coffee and tea, but he himself had received them from R——.

The woman M—— never wanted to keep at home anything of doubtful provenance.

By contrast, Madame W——, a mother of six, was convicted of having fenced chicory, rice, and a can of paint. She claimed that these goods were provided to her by M—— alone.

T——, a cleaner at the Sotteville depot, a father of three whose wife is dying in hospital, persuades us that he didn't steal anything. His testimony entirely concurs with that of M——, but he doesn't address the alleged fencing.

Madame Y—— admits fencing a pair of socks, the ones that Y—— later gave to X——.

A bitter exchange continued for some time between Madame O——, a hideous cow with a face the color of a geranium, and Madame P——, who sobs and strives mightily to prove that she belongs to a higher class. Each blames the other for having brought her oil and herrings.

The latter's husband, P——, isn't employed by the company. He's fifty years old and looks energetic, with graying hair and a heavy mustache, a family man. Previously convicted of assault and battery, he lives on produce from his garden. This garden adjoins a road a few steps from a viaduct. By going under the viaduct, one reaches the other side of the road. (Here again, a map would have been useful.) No place could be better for fencing goods. P—— admits having fenced the goods brought by O—— and X——. He even admitted having once served as lookout, "mostly for my own personal security," he added.

O——'s son, aged fifteen, admits having received from Madame P—— a package of goods but claimed that he didn't know where they came from, and so on.

During the session's second recess the jurors exchanged their impressions as they went off to dinner. For the first time they turned against the district attorney. It was a very clear about-face of opinion and quite strange to observe.

They repeated to one another what was in the reports, that these old employees remained faithful for the whole time that they worked under the direction of the former company. If now they took part in the general disorder, wasn't the new leadership to blame? One of their lawyers said, "When suddenly these men saw the word *Federal* printed on their caps instead of the word *Western*, each of them thought, 'The federal government is myself!' It's not surprising that they permitted themselves a few liberties."[21] No doubt they think that if these people are sentenced, public outcry will be silenced! Unable to nab the true guilty parties—or who knows, perhaps afraid to nab them—they're trying to make these small-time crooks pay in their place. No! No, the jurors won't be so naive as to play along with this game. They won't destroy the careers of these family men, to leave the prosecutors and the noble federal company sitting pretty. Some are already delighting at the thought of the president's expression after the response of the jurors, who were perfectly prepared to vote "not guilty," forcing him to acquit all the prisoners. What a fine end of session that would be! The newspapers would speak of it for sure!

No doubt the president got wind of these inclinations; when he reappeared before us when the session resumed, his face seemed a trifle gloomy. We listened to the cross-examination and the lawyers' speeches. Out of fear that one of us might back out, two supplemental jurors had been named who were ready to fill in, if needed. We took pity on them during the deliberation. Even though we were agreed and all decided in advance, the deliberation lasted more than ninety minutes, the foreman obstinately refusing to group the questions and forcing us to vote

21. Tr. note: "L'état c'est moi": this famous phrase, attributed to the Sun King, Louis XIV (1638–1715), means, "I am the government!"

on almost each one separately. Shut up in a separate small room, the supplemental jurors must have been having a fine time of it! Did they at least have newspapers and cigarettes? We asked the guard on duty to go find out.

One point remained rather delicate: we didn't want to find these pilferers guilty, of course. But on the edge of the bench sat an old witch of a receiver of stolen goods with a faded mop of tousled hair and a hoarse voice, and she didn't deserve to get off. As the district attorney said, citing a well-known adage: the fence makes the thief. Let's show that we have understood and let the punishment fall on the former. We returned to the main room, already quite amused, with smiles of sympathy for the poor supplemental jurors.

The court retired in turn, only to reappear after a moment. The president looked unwelcoming indeed.

"Gentlemen," he said, "I'm sorry to have to point out, on the paper you've given me, a breach of logic that nullifies your vote—no doubt an oversight—which to my great regret will force me to ask you to return to the jury room to agree on your verdicts. You have voted *guilty* of receiving stolen goods and *not guilty* of theft. In order for there to have been receiving of stolen goods, a theft had to occur. It is impossible to receive the results of a theft that has not been committed."

Exactly. But it was this apparent breach of logic that pleased us. We felt we were free to find guilty whomever we pleased; by finding the fence guilty while acquitting the thief, we implied that we suspected there had been fencing of more merchandise than the thefts in question had produced, fencing of other materials, the result of other thefts, committed by those whom the district attorney had not yet arrested. Decidedly, we overestimated our own importance. We were brought back down to a sense of the limits of our powers.

We returned in single file to the small jury room, so sheepishly and with our heads hanging so low that I could barely keep from laughing. The supplemental jurors were also locked up.

We changed our verdict as much as was necessary and reached a compromise that I no longer recall.

Epilogue

Three months later.

The scene takes place in a passenger car between Narbonne, where I left Paul Alibert,[22] and Nîmes.

In a third-class compartment sits a little fellow, around sixteen years old, not bad looking, innocent, smiling at anyone who speaks to him. But he doesn't understand French well, and I don't speak Provençal well.[23] A fortyish woman in deep mourning, with inexpressive features, a foolish gaze, and irremediably childish thoughts, slices flat sausage onto bread and swallows huge mouthfuls. She acts as the stripling's interpreter, and a conversation begins with my neighbor on the right-hand side, a thickhead who grins over his belly at things, people, and life.

Spraying quantities of food around her, the woman explains that the adolescent boy has been summoned from the Perpignan region to Montpellier, where he must testify that very day in court, not at all as a defendant, but as victim. A few days ago some countryside thugs attacked him on the road at midnight and left him for dead in a field after taking the little money he had on him.

We began to speak about criminals:

"Those folks, they should be killed," said the woman.

"You sentence them twenty or thirty times," explained my neighbor; "you support them at the state's expense. All that leads to nothing good. What does society get from it? I ask you, sir, just what does society get?"

Another traveler, who seemed to be sleeping in the corner of the car: "First of all, these folks, once they get out, they never manage to find a place for themselves."

22. Tr. note: François-Paul Alibert (1873–?) was a French poet and author of erotic novels. Gide visited Alibert in November 1912, as is mentioned in Gide's *Correspondance avec François-Paul Alibert (1907–1950)*, ed. Claude Martin (Lyon: Presses Universitaires de Lyon, 1982). See also François-Paul Alibert, *En Italie avec André Gide. Impressions d'Italie (1913): Voyage avec Gide, Ghéon et Rouart*, ed. Daniel Moutote (Lyon: Presses Universitaires de Lyon, 1983). For more on Alibert, see "Hommage à un ami d'André Gide, François-Paul Alibert," *Le Bulletin des amis d'André Gide* 24 (October 1974): 4–46.

23. Tr. note: Provençal, or "Languedocien," is a French Occitan language spoken in the Languedoc Province from Montpellier to Toulouse, Bordeaux, Rodez, and Albi. Mainly heard in rural communities, it resembles the literary variety of Middle Occitan used by medieval troubadours.

The fat gentleman: "But sir, you can understand why no one wants them. They're right. These people, after short time, start all over again."

When the other traveler ventured that there were those who, with support and help, could make acceptable and sometimes good workers, the fat gentleman, who wasn't listening, replied: "The best way to force them to work is to set them to pumping at the bottom of a ditch that's filling up with water; the water rises when they stop pumping. That way they're really forced."

The lady in mourning: "How awful!"

"I'd prefer to kill them right off," moaned another lady.

But when the lady in mourning agreed with her, the woman who had first expressed the opinion, no doubt one of those people who find a snag in their own opinions once they are no longer expressed by themselves, added: "My father, *who was on the jury himself,* used to only give them life sentences. He said that it would give them time to repent."

The fat gentleman shrugged his shoulders. For him, a criminal was a criminal; no use trying to get him away from that.

The lady who had said almost nothing timidly expressed the idea that bad education often played a major part in a criminal's development, and often his parents had primary responsibility.

The fat gentleman thought that after all, education wasn't all-powerful, and some characters were devoted to evil the way others are devoted to doing good.

The gentleman in the corner drew closer and spoke of heredity: "The best education will never win out over the evil bent of an alcoholic's son. Three-quarters of all murderers are the children of alcoholics. Alcoholism . . ."

The lady in mourning interrupted: "Also in Narbonne the women's custom of wearing a black kerchief on their heads. A doctor has discovered that it overheats their brains . . ."

Nevertheless, she did believe there would be fewer crimes if parents weren't so weak.

"One of them was tried in Perpignan," she continued, "and this is how he got started: as a very small child, one day he took a tiny ball of thread from his mother's workbasket. His mother saw it and didn't scold him, so, when the child realized he wouldn't be punished, he continued. He robbed people and then, you understand, finally he murdered people. He was sentenced to death, and here's what he said at the foot of the scaffold (her voice swells, and my overcoat is covered with remnants of her snack): 'Motherrrs and Fatherrrs, I started by stealing a ball of thread, and if my mother had punished me that first time, you wouldn't see me on the scaffold today!' That's what he said, and he had no regrets, except for strangling a tiny baby who had smiled at him in its cradle."

The fat gentleman, who wasn't listening to the lady any more than she'd listened to him, went back to his idea that we don't treat these folk harshly enough: "We'll never make anything good out of them, and if we let them live, it mustn't be for their own pleasure, right? Naturally, these criminals are always complaining, and nothing's good enough for them. I know a story about one who was convicted by mistake. After twenty-seven years, they let him go, because the real guilty man made a complete confession as he was dying. So the son of the man who they convicted by mistake made the trip and brought his father back home from across the sea, and you know what he said when he arrived? That it wasn't so bad down there. Which means, sir, that there are plenty of honest folk in France who are less lucky than criminals are."

"God would have punished him," said the fat lady in mourning, after a pensive silence.

"Who's that?"

"Ah! The real criminal, of course! God is good, but he is fair, you know."

"All the same, I'm really surprised that the priest told about the confession," said the other lady; "they're not allowed to. The secrecy of confession is a holy thing."

"But ma'am, several people heard the confession. When he saw that he was dying, what did he have to lose? On the contrary, he wanted it to be told. That was seven years ago. Twenty-seven years after the crime. Twenty-seven years! Think of it. And nobody suspected anything; he had continued to live as a respected man in his region."

"What was his crime?" asked the gentleman in the corner.

"He had murdered a woman."

Me: "It seems to me, sir, that this example slightly contradicts what you suggested a minute ago."

The fat gentleman turned red: "So you don't believe what I'm telling you?"

"Of course, of course! You don't understand me. I'm simply saying that this example proves that sometimes a man may commit an isolated crime and not rush into new crimes afterward. Look at that man; you say that after his crime he led an honest life for twenty-seven years. Had you convicted him, there is a good chance that you would have made him relapse into crime."

"But sir, the Berenger Law precisely . . . ," began the other lady.

The one in mourning interrupted: "So you don't call that a crime, to let an innocent man go to prison in his place?"

The second gentleman shrugged his shoulders and sank back in his corner. The thickhead fell asleep.

The kid got off at Montpellier. As soon as he left, the lady in mourning, having finished her meal and replaced in her basket the remnants of bread and sausage, commented: "Traveling like that since morning, the child must be hungry!"

Appendix:
Answer to a Survey (*L'Opinion* from October 25, 1913)

"Jurors judge themselves."[24]

No doubt these questions are "in the air." I've spent the last weeks of summer clarifying my assize court memories, which shortly will appear in magazine form and then in a book.

I felt that a simple account of the cases we were called on to judge would be more eloquent than any criticism. However, *L'Opinion*'s survey has made me formulate the following:

It cannot be denied that some of justice's cogwheels occasionally squeak. But today it seems to be believed that the only squeaks come from the jury. At least today, only this aspect is mentioned; I was obliged to conclude more than once, however—and not only at the session in which I sat as a juror—that the machine often squeaks on the side of cross-examinations as well. The examining judge arrives with a firm

24. Tr. note: Gide published an article in the October 25, 1913, issue of the newspaper *L'Opinion* as his contribution to a survey with the overall title "Jurors judge themselves."

opinion of the case, about which the juror still knows nothing. The manner in which the president asks questions, supports and favors the testimony of one witness, even unconsciously, and, by contrast, obstructs and rushes through that of another quickly betrays his personal opinion to the jurors. How hard it is for jurors (I mean provincial jurors) not to be influenced by the president's opinion, either (if they find the president "likable") accepting it or abruptly choosing the opposite view! That's what became clear in more than one case, which, in my memoir, I described without further comment.

It seemed to me that (at least in the cases I had to judge) lawyers' speeches rarely if ever made jurors change their first impressions—to the point where it would hardly be exaggerating to say that a skillful judge can make of a jury whatever he wishes.

Cross-examination by the judge . . . Perhaps another survey by *L'Opinion* will raise this sensitive question another time. Not having attended criminal court sessions in England, I cannot predict whether cross-examination by lawyers and the district attorney might pose even graver problems. In any event, that's not what you've invited me to address today.

My opinion on the composition of a jury? It's that the composition is highly defective. I don't quite know how the one on which I served had been put together, but surely if it was the result of a selection, then it was a reverse selection. I mean to say that all those people from the city or countryside who might have apparently deserved to take part were carefully excluded—if they didn't withdraw, that is.

"And yourself?" I may be asked. Had I not insisted to the mayor of my town, responsible for compiling the first lists, that for the past six years he regularly put my name on them, I'm quite certain he would never have suggested me—*for fear of disturbing me.* After receiving my summons, I still worried about being removed as an *intellectual,* either for the entire session or for each case in turn.

(That's what I was led to fear, and I recalled that my father, called for jury duty, had been systematically eliminated as a juror each time his name was drawn from the box.)

Nothing of the sort occurred. Because some of my colleagues frequently withdrew, I could sit on juries for a great number of cases and more than once witnessed a jury's bafflement, confusion, and panic.

Yet I didn't take part in the case in which the jurors, having voted in such a way that the court had to give the defendant a life sentence at hard labor, and horrified by the result of their vote, gathered immediately after the session and, hurrying from one extreme to another, signed a petition for a full and complete pardon.

It was suggested to us that the jury foreman be named not by drawing lots, as he currently is (the first name drawn from the box), but in the jury room, by vote—as is sometimes done. I think this would be a very apt reform. For I've seen, in certain cases, some jury foremen contribute to the disarray by their uncertainty, incomprehension, and slowness, which a good jury foreman might on the contrary prevent. (In truth, the most inept one was also the proudest of his status and the least willing to give it up.)

Advanced education isn't essential to be a good juror, and I know some "country folk" whose decisions (sometimes a bit stubborn) were more sound than those of a number of intellectuals; nevertheless, I'm astonished that people completely unaccustomed to mental work should be capable of the sustained attention required of them here, for hours at a time. One of them told me about his fatigue; he withdrew from the last sessions: "I'd surely go mad," he said. He was one of the best.

I also believe that a juror's opinion is formed and fixed rather quickly. After a half-hour or forty-five minutes, he's overwhelmed either with doubt or conviction. (I'm speaking of provincial jurors.)

In general, here as elsewhere, the violence of opinions is in proportion to the lack of education and incapacity for critical thinking.

Therefore, if we are in a mood for reform, I feel that the first should be to compile recruitment lists for jurors with the most suitable people, not the idlest and least significant. Moreover, these people must swear not to get themselves excused.

I recently heard a proposal that the jury be called to deliberate with the court and to rule on sentences with it. Yes, perhaps. It is troubling that jurors may be surprised by the court's decision and think, We would have voted differently if we could have foreseen that our vote would have resulted in such a heavy—or light—sentence.

Above all it must be said that the questions to which the jury must respond are posed in such a way that they often appear as a trap, forcing the unfortunate juror to vote against the truth to arrive at what he feels to be just.

More than once I've seen honest country people, resolved not to vote for aggravating circumstances, faced by the questions, did the theft occur at night? . . . with assault and battery? . . . by several people? (which would in fact constitute aggravating circumstances), desperately exclaiming, "No matter what, I can't say yes." Then they'd vote for extenuating circumstances, haphazardly, as a stopgap measure.

If the questions cannot be posed differently (and I confess that I don't easily see how they could be posed), it would be good if, at the start of the first session, the jurors received some instructions that might forestall their anguish and confusion—instructions about the sentences to which their votes would lead.

It has been suggested that a separate copy of the page of questions be given to each one of them before the session starts; this step seems to me to offer genuine advantages—and no disadvantages that I can see.

I'd also propose that in certain cases, a topographical map be given to each of the jurors, allowing him to more easily imagine the scene of the crime. In one case concerning an attack by night, for which I was called to serve, the jurors' certainty depended wholly on this question: was the defendant close enough to a streetlight and sufficiently well lit so that Madame X—— might have identified him from her window? One witness, called to the bar, situated the streetlight at five meters away, and another at twenty-five meters from the exact spot of the attack. A third went so far as to claim that there was no streetlight at all in this part of the street. Wouldn't it have been simpler for the police to draft a map of the site?

Monsieur Bergson asks that each juror be required to justify and explain his vote.[25] Of course, but I wasn't at all convinced that the juror who is the clumsiest at speech is the one who feels and thinks the least ably. And vice versa, alas!

25. Tr. note: The philosopher Henri Bergson (1859–1941) replied to a survey about the judicial system in the October 19, 1913, issue of *Le Temps,* arguing that if jurors could be given more responsibility for their decisions, they would prove less indulgent.

❦ ❦ ❦ The Redureau Case

Preface

The series of books of which this is the first volume[1] is in no way an anthology of Famous Cases. What interest us are not "cunning crimes" but rather the "cases," not necessarily criminal, whose grounds remain mysterious, escaping the laws of traditional psychology, and confound human justice, which, when it tries to apply its logic of *Is fecit cui prodest*,[2] risks being swept into severe mistakes. For example, the Redureau case, which is described here, shows us a gentle, well-behaved child, acknowledged as perfectly healthy in body and mind, born of healthy and honest parents, who, without our being able to understand why, suddenly cuts the throats of seven people. "Normal psychology," the expert doctors would say—that is, not pathological. Yet the motives of this abominable act are neither greed, jealousy, hatred, rejected love, nor indeed anything that one could easily recognize and catalog.

Surely no human act is entirely unmotivated; no act is gratuitous, except in appearance. But we must agree here that current psychological expertise doesn't allow us to understand everything and that there are many unexplored regions, or *terrae incognitae,* on the map of the human soul. The purpose of this series of books is to attract attention to these and help to better glimpse what is only beginning to be suspected.

For the cases to be described, we'll furnish as much information as possible, without fear of boring the reader. We aim not to amuse but to instruct. We will set ourselves before the facts like a naturalist, not a

---

1. Ed. note: The subject here is the series of books, *Judge Not,* published under the direction of André Gide, of which the first volume appeared in 1930.

2. Tr. note: The Roman playwright Seneca wrote, "Cui prodest scelus, is fecit"—the one who derives advantage from the crime is the likeliest to have committed it.

painter or novelist. A story is often all the more moving for being suc-
cinct, but we are not concerned with effects. We will present, while
doing our best to stand aside, as authentic a documentation as possible;
by that I mean not interpretations but direct testimony.

We are aware of the difficulties of this venture. Documents of this
kind are less scarce than they are difficult to produce; thus we call on
all those interested by these questions, who may be able to mail us or
point out significant ones.

1

On September 30, 1913, young Marcel Redureau, a fifteen-year-old servant in the employ of Monsieur and Madame Mabit, farmers in the
Charente-Inférieure region, savagely murdered the entire Mabit family and the servant Marie Dugast, a total of seven persons.

First, let's briefly recall the facts. The best is to quote the part of the
indictment that states the crime:

"On October 1, 1913, around seven o'clock in the morning, Madame
Durant, a housewife in Bas-Briacé, who usually went every day to buy
milk from Monsieur and Madame Mabit, her neighbors, was quite astonished to find that their house was silent and closed up.

"On the doorstep, dissolved in tears and dressed only in his shirt, sat
little Pierre Mabit, four years old. When questioned, the child said that
his mother was inside the house, where she was bleeding, as well as his
grandmother.

"Because Madame Durant knew that Madame Mabit was in an advanced state of pregnancy, she thought it was a premature childbirth
and went away unobtrusively. She repeated the child's words to Monsieur Gohaud, who came to the house in turn, and pushing the window shutters, which were still half-open, he observed, stretched out on
the floor of the room and lying in a pool of blood, the lifeless bodies
of Madame Mabit and Marie Dugast, her maid. Another neighbor, a
certain Monsieur Aubron, having arrived unexpectedly, joined Gohaud,
and the two men entered the kitchen, where they saw that the victims'
throats had been cut. Without stopping to check on what might have
happened to the house's other occupants, Aubron rode his bicycle to

the gendarmes' headquarters at Louroux-Bottereau. Two men from the squad immediately went to the village of Bas-Briacé and entered the Mabit house, where a terrifying sight greeted them. They found that in fact there were not two victims but seven, and the throat of every member of the Mabit family, with the exception of little Pierre, had been cut, along with that of the young maid, Marie Dugast.

"All the bodies were horribly mutilated, and the evidence was clear that the murderer, not satisfied with just killing, had attacked his victims with such savagery that it was impossible to count the stab wounds, they were so numerous and close together.

. . . .

"The gendarmes, surprised not to find the servant Marcel Redureau, who also worked for Monsieur and Madame Mabit, anywhere in the house, began a search and found him in an unoccupied house near his parent's home, around five hundred meters from the crime scene. Since he had traces of blood on his face and shirt, he was arrested, and after some hesitating, he confessed that he alone committed all the murders.

"During the whole preliminary investigation, Marcel Redureau stuck to the confession he had made to the police officers, and in various interrogations, he offered without visible emotion details about the circumstances in which he committed the crimes.

"Around 10 P.M. on September 30 he and Mabit were working together at the winepress. The boss held the bar that activates the press's vise, while Redureau, standing on the platform, helped him in the job and backed up his efforts. Since the servant showed little eagerness for the task, Mabit told him he was a lazybones and that for several days he had been dissatisfied with him.

"At this remark, the irked Redureau stepped down from the winepress, armed himself with a wooden hammer, a kind of fifty-centimeter-long bludgeon that was within his reach, and struck several blows at the head of his master, who sank down groaning, letting go of the bar. Then, seeing that he was still alive, Redureau grabbed a huge chopper that the country folk call a grape billhook, which is used not on vines but rather to separate bunches of grapes that are piled in the winepress.

"This weapon, which must be seen to understand the terrible wounds it can make, is made up of a sharp blade, rounded at the tip, that weighs around two and a half kilos and measures sixty-five centimeters long by thirteen wide; it is backed by a wooden handle about a meter long.[3]

"Using this instrument, Redureau opened the throat of his master, who was in his final agony and soon gave his last gasp.

"The defendant stated that, the first crime done, he initially meant to flee, but while heading for the kitchen to return the winepress lantern, he was challenged by Madame Mabit, who was doing mending work with Marie Dugast and who asked him what had become of her husband. Fearing that she might go into the winepress room, where she would have found the corpse, Redureau decided to eliminate all witnesses to the crime, to be sure of impunity. Without answering Madame Mabit, but carrying out his idea, the defendant returned to the winepress; there he took the bloody chopper he had just used and returned to the kitchen, where he murdered the two women.

"The grandmother either had not yet fallen asleep or was awakened by the tragedy occurring a few steps away from her, and she must have gone to help her daughter-in-law. She had to die in turn. So, without wasting time, lighting his way with a lantern, his chopper in hand, Redureau suddenly rose up in front of her and killed her.

"This left three children, whose horrified screams might have attracted the neighbors' attention. They were all sacrificed; the two-year-old child, who might have seemed too young to concern the criminal, was not spared any more than were the rest, and Redureau struck him with such ferocity that, as he himself admitted, he broke the handle of the chopper on the last victim's cradle.

"Little Pierre Mabit, who was sleeping in the kitchen and who, either terrorized or asleep, did not cry out, was for that reason excluded from the shocking butchery.

3. Given the weapon Redureau used, the wounds could not have been superficial. This weapon, "with more aspects of a scythe or ax" than of a knife, had a swing that easily explains the depth of the injuries. Clearly Redureau had lost all control and must have hit out wildly. At first I sought proof of his momentary unawareness in the fact that his weapon broke at precisely the moment when he was massacring his most vulnerable victim, who could have offered the least resistance; after consideration, however, it seemed to me that the grape knife's long handle could have struck an iron or wooden post on the cradle in which the two-year-old child doubtless slept.

"Redureau carefully replaced his murder instrument in the winepress room, where it was found the next day, and after placing the blood-stained lantern on the curb of the courtyard well, he returned to his room, where he spent the rest of the night. In the morning he headed for his parents' house.

"He stated that he felt remorse and thought of drowning himself in a nearby body of water; as it happened, however, this was a passing whim, and one may wonder whether he hadn't just planned to wet his shoes and the bottom of his pants to make his sham suicide look more realistic.[4]

"The accused belonged to a large, respectable family. He had worked only a few months for Monsieur and Madame Mabit. He was intelligent, having earned a primary-school diploma, but according to certain witnesses appeared uncommunicative, with a shifty and spiteful personality. If we are to believe a certain Monsieur Chiron, who met him in the middle of July and congratulated him on his new job with the honest Monsieur and Madame Mabit, Marcel Redureau replied with a solemnity that later events would justify: 'I don't like them; they ought to be killed. If it was up to me, I'd kill them all. I wouldn't leave one alive.'"

A few remarks on the subject of the singular testimony of this Monsieur Chiron. The statements he made suggest, if not exactly a premeditated crime, at least a certain inclination to commit one, which would greatly lessen its strangeness. Based on a careful examination of the trial records that an *N.R.F.*[5] reader kindly obtained for me (and I'd like to thank him cordially here), it seems to me that these statements are sheer invention. That the president of the tribunal nevertheless felt obliged to take them into account is one thing. It is shocking that the district attorney, wanting to measure the credibility of Monsieur Chiron's testimony, summoned before the jury only character witnesses who

4. The forensic pathologists did not share the district attorney's skepticism. On this point (the suicide attempt) as on all the others, Redureau—who in no way tried to extenuate his guilt—seemed perfectly sincere to them.

Let's observe as well that Redureau, after his murders were committed, did not for a single moment think of taking from the cupboard the money that was surely there and that might have helped him to flee. Not for a single moment did he think of fleeing.

5. Tr. note: *N.R.F.* is the *Nouvelle revue française,* a periodical published by Gallimard that Gide helped to establish.

praised Monsieur Chiron while ignoring the other ones, along with his strict duty. It is noteworthy that the few people favorable to Chiron, among those whom the gendarmes visited, were (1) a pork butcher to whom Monsieur Chiron sold his hogs, (2) a butcher to whom Monsieur Chiron sold other animals for slaughter, and (3) yet another tradesman with whom Monsieur Chiron had done business for years. The other witnesses, whose testimony was of a kind to greatly modify the jurors' opinion, would have depicted Monsieur Chiron as perhaps a man of honor but also a "braggart" and "inventive."

One of them said, "Monsieur Chiron has a special cast of mind that leads him to talk about imaginary things. He loves to give himself a role in the major events of the region." Regarding a certain epoch-making regional law from 1898, Chiron went so far as to claim that it was passed thanks to him. He said that he had made available to the inquest a document that turned out to be decisive for the vote. Regarding the crime of September 30, 1913, which was also a momentous event in the local history of Landreau, Chiron didn't think of the phrase at first, not reporting or inventing it until two days later. At first he expressed the opinion that the crime could have been committed only by a foreigner.

Let's also add this. I've just stated that none of the witnesses unfavorable to Chiron had been summoned; I was mistaken. Mr. Pierre Bertin, who testified, as I previously noted, on Chiron's "odd cast of mind," was called, but only in error. Here's how it happened: there were two Pierre Bertins at the preliminary investigation; one was a favorable witness, and he was the one whom the district attorney intended to have heard. When the other Pierre Bertin, an unfavorable witness, appeared unexpectedly, Monsieur Chiron showed intense annoyance and hastened to make himself scarce.

Let me be clear: in no way do I presume to lessen the atrocity of Redureau's crime, but when a case is this serious, we have the right to expect that even the prosecution will be resolved to present for justice's sake all appurtenances, even those that might be favorable to the defendant—above all when he is an impoverished child, with no help other than a public defender.

I've stressed this point also because the psychological interest of the Redureau case would be much diminished were it proven that the idea for the crime had long possessed the young murderer's mind, as the apocryphal statements would lead us to believe. Furthermore, it is noteworthy that this is the only point about which Redureau protested vehemently, otherwise making a full confession immediately, admitting his guilt of everything of which he was accused.[6] But he never expressed these words; before committing the crime, he never had the idea of committing it.

2

1. Mr. Henry Barby writes in *Le Journal* (Saturday, October 4, 1913):

Nantes, October 3d (dispatch from our special correspondent).—Yesterday I pointed out at the end of my article that people here were refusing to believe that a simple remark by his employer could have been enough, as Marcel Redureau claimed it was, to turn him into a savagely cruel murderer of seven persons.

Indeed, this fifteen-year-old kid had *none of the hereditary disfigurations,*[7] none of the stigmata of degeneracy, that characterize the born criminal. Marcel Redureau was the fourth of ten children, all energetic, healthy, and respectable like their parents. These people, small-farm owners, produced both crops and wine and lived on what they raised. Their home was located scarcely three hundred meters from the Mabit farm. They are respected in the area, and their children received nothing but good advice and good examples from them.

Their son Marcel-Joseph-René, whose horrific, heinous crime had just plunged them into despair, was born on June 24, 1896. Therefore he was exactly fifteen years and three months old. His childhood was uneventful, like that of any little country boy who, barely having reached the age of reason, goes out to earn his bread to help his family.

The mayor of Landreau, Monsieur de Boisgueheneuc, who knew him well, could not understand how he could have committed the crime:

"Marcel," he declared, "whose family lived on excellent terms with the Mabits, never gave any cause until now for anyone to fear him. Perhaps

6. Also noteworthy are the newspapers' inaccuracy on this point as on so many others: "*Today Redureau claims that he never made these remarks, but numerous witnesses have just sworn to the contrary.*" (*Le Journal,* March 1914).

7. All italics are my own.

he was a little nervous, but that's all. Now they say he is shifty and a loner, but I declare that no one ever noticed it beforehand. He did not drink; in short, nothing could have led us to believe that he was capable of committing such a heinous crime."

His former schoolmaster, Monsieur Béranger, expressed himself similarly:

"Of average intelligence," he said, "Redureau was always well behaved. He was a good student whom I found entirely satisfactory. When he received a reprimand, he never rebelled. He was a rather docile child."

At age eleven Marcel earned his diploma and left school. His parents looked for a job for him. A little too frail to start off working for strangers, he tended livestock for his uncle, Monsieur Louis Bouyer, a farmer at Bonnières, two kilometers away from Landreau. Quite well behaved, neither lazy nor sulky, he continued working for three years for his uncle, who was entirely pleased with him.

After having worked ten months for his family, Marcel Redureau was hired last June as a servant at the Mabit farm, where he replaced his older brother, who left for army service. His annual wages were three hundred and sixty francs.

"He was so timid," his father states, "that he didn't dare go out in the evening."

What happened during the last three months to transform this shy, gentle, fearful lad into a blood-intoxicated brute?

As soon as the crime was revealed, robbery was thought to be the motive. The previous Sunday Monsieur Mabit had withdrawn 3,000 francs, his earnings from the sale of part of the harvest. Although the money was available to the murderer, it was later found untouched. Therefore(!) Marcel had killed only for revenge.

Now that the horrible image of the crime began to dim, people were talking and tongues wagged at Landreau and the village of Bas-Briacé, and from these rumors an unexpected account emerged.

Marcel Redureau apparently became aware of the budding charms of Marie Dugast, the farmers' young maid. Like him, Marie had worked for Monsieur and Madame Mabit for the past three months.

Now, it was said in the village that on the day of the crime, Marcel Redureau had tried to rape the young maid, who was fifteen years old, like himself, and his act drew a sharp scolding from Madame Mabit. The farmer would have added his own strict and justified admonitions to those of his wife. But was this true?

Be that as it may, it is the judicial inquiry's turn to speak. Monsieur Mallet, the examining magistrate responsible for investigating the crime, wrote to the leader of the bar attached to the court of Nantes, asking him to appoint a lawyer to aid Marcel Redureau. The leader named the lawyer Abel Durand.

Henry Barby

(*Le Journal,* Saturday, October 4, 1913)

2. The correspondent for *Le Temps* writes to his paper:

The funerals for the victims of the crime at Landreau were held yesterday at three o'clock, amid a substantial crowd. The justice of the peace affixed the official seals on the home of the deceased.

The mayor of Landreau declared that he knew Redureau very well and that nothing warned of this sort of predisposition in the young man. He wasn't shifty or a loner, as some liked to claim now. He even had some friends. He didn't drink.

For some time, however, Redureau had drawn some comments from his employer. Perhaps these comments irritated him to the point of making him lose his head.

Moreover, Redureau's former schoolmaster declared that although of average intelligence, he was a good student, whom he found entirely satisfactory. He had successfully received his school diploma. The teacher, too, had been very surprised by the news of the crime.

The pathologists stated that they had rarely seen such relentlessness. It was impossible for them to discern, on some of the corpses, the order of the wounds and their exact number. Redureau must have struck the seven people whom he killed a total of fifty or sixty times.

The weapon he used is a grape billhook measuring fifty centimeters. The handle is longer than the blade. The blade is curved like a Turkish saber, resembling a yataghan.

The murderer spent a very quiet night in the Nantes prison. Not having a defense attorney yet, he probably won't be interrogated until Monday.

(*Le Temps,* October 4, 1913)

3. *Le Temps* published the following further information:

Our correspondent in Nantes writes:
The leader of the bar attached to the legal association named Abel

Durand as Marcel Redureau's defense attorney. Redureau fell under the application of articles 66 and 67 of the penal code, which reads as follows:

Art. 66.—When a defendant is younger than sixteen years old, and if it is decided that he acted without proper judgment, he will be acquitted but will, according to the circumstances, be returned to his parents' custody or sent to a correctional facility, to be held there and raised for a period of time that shall not go beyond his twentieth birthday.

Art. 67.—If, on the contrary, the defendant acted with proper judgment, a distinction must be made according to the penalty that shall be imposed on him. If it be a death penalty, or a life sentence at hard labor, he shall be sentenced to ten to twenty years' imprisonment in a correctional facility. If he incurs a sentence of a finite period of hard labor or imprisonment, he shall be sentenced to imprisonment in a correctional facility for a period equal to at least one-third and not exceeding one-half the time for which he would have been sentenced.

Therefore, the worst sentence that the criminal of Landreau may incur is twenty years' imprisonment.

The possible motives have disappeared one by one after the crime. Theft was considered, because Redureau's employer received 2,000 francs on Sunday from the sale of his wine. The money was found untouched, and this hypothesis set aside. The idea of a crime of passion also seems not to have been worthy of retaining. Revenge is left, Redureau's resentment against his employer who scolded him. It seems that the examining magistrate will point the investigation in this direction.

While waiting, the accused always looks quite calm, apparently unaware of the horrible crime that he has committed. He eats and sleeps well and does not appear to be obsessed by remorse. On Friday afternoon he was visited by his lawyer, with whom he had a fairly long conversation.

(*Le Temps*, October 5, 1913)

3. Pathologist's Report

Now I will allow the pathologists (Messrs. Cullerre and Desclaux) to speak. Their report is so significant that I trust others may be grateful if it is quoted nearly in its entirety:

"What characterizes this horrible tragedy is that its source assumes none of the habitual etiological conditions of juvenile crime. It was neither the product of heredity nor the influence of environment: its perpetrator had no hereditary evil antecedents; he was raised in an irreproachable environment and was given only good lessons and examples. Nor was it the result of one of those regressive defects so common to young criminals: instinctive evil-mindedness, psychic anesthesia, and absence of moral feeling. Indeed, nothing in the young murderer's preliminary psychological report permits this hypothesis. It is remarkable that none of the people at the hearing among whom or near whom he grew up described him as a mentally degenerate child. All those who knew him or associated with him agreed that he was very intelligent and industrious, with no known defects. However, one point of certain importance is worth stressing: the witnesses were nearly unanimous in attributing to him a withdrawn personality, slightly disobedient and shifty.[8]

"Nor is he a degenerate in the somatic sense of the word, despite the far-fetched descriptions that may be read in some of the newspaper reports of the trial. 'This boy,' wrote one of them, 'is practically a child whose physical development is not yet complete. If the railing that separates the defendant's box from the courtroom floor weren't latticework, he wouldn't be visible sitting down, and when standing he is as tall as a bale of hay.' In fact, Redureau measures 1 meter, 584, or five centimeters above Quételet's average for sixteen-year-old boys.[9] The same newspaper continues in this manner: 'His head is big, with locks of blond hair that fall on a low, bulging forehead. His profile is recessive, with a straight nose over a widely stretched mouth.'[10] Not one of these details is correct or corresponds with reality. His forehead is neither low nor particularly bulging and not at all receding. The head and face, taken together, are very evenly proportioned; not the slightest sign of Morel's stigma is to

8. Another personality trait that I am surprised was not mentioned here, and to which I will return later: Marcel Redureau, according to some, was fearful, with a fear that might be attributed to excessive "irritability."

9. Tr. note: Lambert Adolphe Quételet (1796–1874) was a Belgian astronomer and statistician whose book *Sur l'homme et le développement de ses facultés, essai d'une physique sociale* (1835) proposed his notion of the average man as a standard with regular, quantifiable variations. He also studied crime statistics and was involved in judicial reform.

10. The newspaper in question happens to be *Le Temps* (October 2, 1913), and I seek no better example of the kind of errors that can be caused by prejudice.

be seen.[11] The same error appears with respect to the ears, described as 'enormous' by the article in question. They are, according to the anthropometrical record, 6.8 centimeters high; they are absolutely symmetrical, well-proportioned, normally edged, and do not stand out from the skull. The only distinctive feature they offer is the presence of Darwin's tubercle, which is no doubt exceptional but not a disorder.[12]

"Another newspaper was closer to the truth when it made the following portrait of the murderer: 'Blond, even very blond, with blue eyes, he is a rather nice boy; he is far from having the brute's face that we generally attribute to murderers.'[13]

"He's a withdrawn, shifty boy: that's all that could be found to explain his crime. And yet, before that day, apparently no one complained about his personality. His family never saw him in this light, nor did the schoolteacher who taught him for six years.

"No doubt the determining circumstances of this frightful butchery are the impulsiveness of the climacteric years of adolescence and the powerful instrument of death, called a grape cutter in this region, which is like a scythe or ax and happened to be within arm's reach.

"The crime committed by young Redureau is one of the most horrific that can be imagined. On September 20, 1913, around 10:30 P.M., while he was busy at the winepress with his employer, the latter having made some criticisms of his work, he clubbed him with a hammer and slit his throat with the grape cutter. He then went to the family residence, where he successively killed in the same manner Madame Mabit, her servant, her mother-in-law, and three of her children, attacking the victims with unbelievable violence. We will not offer any further detailed description of the tragedy here but will study all its circumstances later.

"We have collected from the accused's own family the following information about his past history, both hereditary and personal:

11. Tr. note: Benedict-Auguste Morel (1809–73), author of *Traité des dégénérescences physiques, intellectuelles et morales de l'espèce humaine et des causes qui produisent ces variétés maladies* (1857), was a pioneer in biopsychiatry who proposed biological causes—such as genes or brain chemistry—for mental illness or "degeneracy."

12. Tr. note: Darwin's tubercle is a slight projection on the edge of the human ear that some scientists assume to be a remnant of the pointed ears of quadrupeds—also called the auricular tubercle by Charles Darwin, who included a diagram of it in his *Descent of Man* (1871).

13. *Le Phare de la Loire,* October 2, 1913.

"There was no illness either convulsive or insane in the direct ancestry or among forebears or collateral relatives on either side. Nor were there eccentrics, odd individuals, or alcoholics.

"The father and mother are healthy and robust. They have suffered no serious illness that could affect their physical constitution or brain functions.

"They had eleven children, of whom ten are still alive, six boys and four girls. The eldest, a daughter, is twenty-one years old, and the youngest is twenty months old. The third child, a boy, died four days after birth. The accused is the fifth in order of age. His mother's pregnancies and childbirths were normal. None of the children suffered serious illnesses, whether general or involving the nervous system or brain functions. They are all robust and never caused any concern about their health.

"Apart from a few minor childhood ailments, Marcel, the accused, had no other illnesses except for an attack of rheumatism in September 1912; when he was working for Monsieur B——, he developed a fever and joint pain, concentrated in the knees, which nevertheless did not swell up. He was ill for only eight days and was back at work two weeks after the ailment began.

"He is intelligent and received his primary-school diploma. He never gave anyone any sort of trouble, neither his employers nor his playmates or people of the region. He never showed any evil instincts. He was not aggressive and was never observed to be cruel to animals.

"His parents admit that he is a little nervous, lively, and impish but never nasty. He is fearful in the general meaning of the term.[14] On this

14. Some witnesses have insisted on Redureau's inclination to fear, which I must say struck me particularly. I was able to observe, while training a nervous and cowardly dog, how his fear was naturally transformed into viciousness. The dog, leaping up at the least unexpected noise, immediately went into a defensive posture. I readily believe that with Redureau, fear made him lose his head to this degree. If, as Agassiz eloquently points out (*On Classification in Zoology*), embryology is of extraordinary use in explaining certain previously unsuspected relationships between animal species that are very different in appearance, I believe that in the same way, it can be particularly instructive to study certain feelings at the embryonic state, so to speak. [Tr. note: The great American naturalist Louis Agassiz (1807–73) wrote *Essay on Classification* (1859). Its French edition was *De l'espèce et de la classification en zoologie,* trans. Félix Vogeli (1869).] Fear is doubtless the embryo of that brief insanity that led Redureau to his crime. A nephew of mine, who acted heroically during the war, remains convinced that the same feeling of fear can madden a soldier until it moves him to acts analogous to that of young Redureau, acts that would earn him the Croix de Guerre.

point, as well as on his personality, they cannot offer any more details. Marcel had no taste for dissipation, didn't drink, and spent his off days playing with his friends. They absolutely never observed that he had an excessive taste for reading. He had spent the previous Sunday with them, and they hadn't noticed anything strange about him. He had never complained to them about his employer, Mabit. The crime deeply amazed them, and they found no way to explain it.

"If we compare this information with information in the procedural file coming from either officials or witnesses questioned at the preliminary hearing, we observe that they do not differ on any major point.

"The justice of the peace of Loroux-Bottereau, in the information report he issued about the accused, declared that he was not known to have any basic flaws, but his personality was 'a bit nervous, sometimes shifty.'

"The schoolmaster who taught him testified: Marcel Redureau was of slightly above average intelligence, a good student, rarely punished. While he attended school, he never gave any cause for complaint. He had a fairly good disposition and did not seem to be shifty. He was well-behaved. He provoked no criticism of his honesty or morals.

"None of the witnesses' testimony differs noticeably from that of the schoolmaster's, except on one point: his personality.

"The witness B——, his uncle, who housed him from age eleven to fourteen, had no complaints about him but said he was untalkative and had a shifty personality.

"The witness C——, the uncle's neighbor, who knew Marcel very well, testified that he was well-behaved and a good worker but had a 'very withdrawn' personality and often failed to answer when he was spoken to.

"The witness Br——, for whom he worked, declared that he was very intelligent but found him to be 'a shifty personality, very independent.'

"All the other witnesses insist on the defendant's special character, but no one provided negative information about his inclinations or morals.

"Madame Br——, wife of the previous witness, made no criticism about his personality, work, or behavior and did not at all see him as violent.

"There was one deposition that, if accurate, clearly brings out Marcel Redureau's character flaws: it's the one by the witness Ch——. Having met the accused around mid-July and knowing that he was hired by the Mabits, he congratulated him, as these people were 'well set up.' But the accused replied: 'I don't like them; they ought to be killed. If it was up to me, I'd kill them all. I wouldn't leave one alive.' The witness adds that Redureau 'spoke in a very cruel tone and seemed to be filled with rage.' This statement, made in anger, would indubitably reveal violent, vindictive premeditation. But we must not forget that the accused energetically denies having said it.

"In sum, the only notice taken of Redureau's mind involves his character. Even on this point, there is no unanimity. The schoolmaster, well placed to evaluate the personality of a child whom he could follow for five or six years, did not see him as shifty; similarly, his father refused to admit 'that he was shifty or vindictive.'

"Madame Br——, one of the aforementioned witnesses, remarked that he read a lot, although she could not say what he read. The witness J—— said in his deposition: 'Only today I learned that he habitually read wicked things,' no doubt a mere echo of the previous witness's testimony. We have been able to ascertain, in any event, that this point was not noteworthy, for Redureau read only a local newspaper and an almanac. He notably never read popular novels whose preferred subjects are crime and murder.

"Redureau was fifteen years and four months old on the day he committed the murders of which he was accused. He is a boy of 1 meter, 584 centimeters in height, with a healthy appearance and normal look, without clear signs of degeneracy. There is no deformation of the skull or the roof of the mouth. His ears are well-formed. His heart and lungs are healthy; the spleen and liver are of normal size. The muscular system is rather well developed; movement, in general, poses no problem. General sensitivity, in its different aspects of touch, pain, heat, and cold, is intact. The sensory organs are not the basis of any anomaly; notably, the sense of color is not altered. Reflexes, examined by the usual clinical method, correspond to the physiological condition.

"His attitude before us is that of an intimidated child. It is difficult to get him to raise his eyes. He speaks at first in a quiet voice, using almost exclusively monosyllabic words; by insisting, however, it is possible to obtain more explicit answers. During his long detention the prison staff noticed nothing unusual about him from a mental point of view, except that he would easily assume a sullen, sulky look when remarks were made to him. He participates in the communal life and conforms to the rules like the other prisoners.

"His moral sensitivity is not disturbed. He sheds tears when reminded of his mother or his brother who has just gone to Algeria for army duty. On the subject of the acts he committed, he expresses regrets that seem sincere. We will see later that he is not immune to remorse.

"He answers pertinently all the questions asked of him. He is well-oriented in time and space. By his words, he shows intelligence and good basic knowledge of history, geography, grammar, and arithmetic. All the answers that he gives us about his past life, employers, work, and salaries are correct or plausible.

"He never drank excessively and was never tipsy, so it's impossible to say how he might act if by chance he became drunk. He met with boys of his age on Sundays to play cards; the winnings or losses never exceeded ten sous. He never went to taverns.

"He never associated with girls and never had sexual intercourse. He was friendly with his employer's young maid but felt nothing special for her and never courted her.

"He never felt emotional torments and never had either an obsession or idée fixe. Whatever our questions of this kind, we receive only complete denials.

"As his father already pointed out, however, he admits that he is fearful. At night he's afraid of the dark, and he doesn't know whether he would be able to run a late errand far from home. If he had been ordered to do so, 'he wouldn't have wanted to go there'; it was a vague and imprecise impression, which was not at all willed or systematic, nor did it correspond to what psychiatry calls a phobia; he didn't believe in ghosts, wouldn't be afraid to walk by a cemetery, wasn't afraid of witches, and didn't know of any in his region. In a word, he was fearful, plain and simple, perhaps in an excessive way for a boy of his age;

nevertheless, although this may indicate nervousness, it is not a relevant sign of pathology.

"Asked about his feelings toward his employer and his family, he formally declared that he never had any complaints about them, nor did he have any feelings of rancor or hatred for them. He got along well with his employer's wife and the young servant girl. Only after the harvest did his employer sometimes speak loudly and insult him. He formally denied the statement that the witness Ch—— attributed to him, to the effect that he felt long-standing resentment and nursed plans for vengeance against them.

"We persisted in trying to find out whether he had drunk an excessive amount of wine on the day of the crime to keep up his strength. His answers at various times were always the same, showing that he drank wine only as permitted at table and in normal quantities, around two glasses with each meal; it was red wine. On rare occasions, before the evening meal, he drank two mouthfuls of white wine along with his employer. This information agrees with the facts provided by the preliminary investigation. Indeed, a one-third-empty bottle of white wine was found in the storeroom. Therefore he affirmed, and we believe that the matter can be considered resolved, that he was not under the influence of alcohol-induced excitement at the time of the tragedy.

"His explanations of the crime remain the same. His employer Mabit and he were working the winepress. Mabit was at the bar, and Redureau was on the platform to repair the vise. Because he didn't finish the work he'd been ordered to do quickly enough, his boss made a scene, shouting 'that he was a blunderer, a lazybones, who for the past eight days hadn't done his work well.' That's went he came down from the winepress and, arming himself with the hammer that was within arm's reach, hit Mabit on the head from behind. Mabit let go of the bar and fell to the ground. As he was groaning, Redureau, after looking at him for a moment, grabbed the grape cutter (a long and wide, sharp blade, 65 centimeters long and 13 wide, weighing around 2.5 kilograms) and cut his throat.

"Next, he took the lantern and went toward the house, where he expected to find everyone in bed. On arriving in the kitchen, however, he saw Madame Mabit and the servant girl, who were working at the table.

At first he intended to flee, but when his employer's wife asked where her husband was, he left without answering. He went to grab the grape cutter, which remained in the storeroom, returned, and struck first the servant and then Madame Mabit. Their backs were to him; they didn't have time to say anything and screamed only at the moment they were hit. He said, 'I hit the servant girl in the neck. She fell down right away, and I also hit my boss's wife on the neck, and she fell down. When she was on the ground, I stabbed her in the stomach.' The grandmother slept in one of the two neighboring rooms, and in the other slept three of the children, who were awakened by the noise and started to scream. So he took the lantern and went first to the grandmother, striking her in the throat: 'She didn't say anything; she didn't have time.' Then he went into the other room: 'I stabbed the throat of one of the crying little girls, and her sister, who was sleeping next to her, woke up at that moment, and I stabbed her as well. The child who was sleeping in his cradle woke up from the noise and began to cry too, so I killed him.'[15] At the last blow the tool's handle broke. Redureau brought the pieces to the storeroom near the winepress, where they were discovered later. Only a little boy, who was sleeping in the kitchen, escaped the butchery.

"The explanation that the accused gives for the horrible tragedy is always the same: in killing his employer, he gave in to a violent rage. Once the murder was done, when he returned to the house, he was very upset, not knowing very well what he was doing. When the boss's wife asked where her husband was, he lost his head. The idea came to him that she would go to the storeroom and discover his crime, so he wanted to get rid of all the witnesses.

"Here are his literal responses: 'I was afraid that my boss's wife would come to see her husband in the storeroom. . . . I hit the servant girl because she was with my boss's wife. . . . I hit the others because they were screaming.' The truth of these responses seems to be corroborated by the following, which attests to its sincerity: 'I didn't touch little Pierre because he didn't make any noise and he was sleeping.'

"On the subject of the multiplicity and violence of the blows dealt

---

15. To go from one room to another, he lit the way with the lantern from the winepress, which he brought along, the lamp that provided light for his employer's wife and the servant girl having been knocked over at the beginning of the tragedy.

to the victims (fractured skulls, chopped faces and necks, severed spinal cords), he could offer no explanation; he also could not say why he had opened the belly of Madame Mabit, who was pregnant and near term. He just protested that he wasn't obeying any obscene or sadistic compulsion. The act was the same sort as the others and resulted merely from anger.

"When he replaced the blade and its broken handle in the storeroom, he went up to his room and sat down. Slowly he regained his self-control and realized the seriousness of what he had just done. Then he felt regret. 'I felt remorse,' he said, 'and I wanted to kill myself.' He had been in his room for about an hour when he went down, intending to drown himself in a pond that was fifty meters from the house. He went into the water and took a few steps, but his courage failed him, and he returned to his room; he stayed there until morning twilight. Then he went back to his parent's place, where he was arrested.

"The suicide attempt seems plausible. It jibes with the remorse felt by the accused, and it seems proven by the fact that a wet pair of pants were discovered in his room. In short, his version seemed sincere. Everything fit together in a logical way, and he didn't try to lessen his own guilt.

"Moreover, it seemed to us to establish clearly that he was fully aware of the deeds that were done and his responsibility. He felt remorse, which means that he knew right from wrong, all the more because he was of an intelligence not just normal for his age but even above average, according to the schoolmaster who taught him. Therefore, there can be no doubt on the question of judgment, in the legal sense of the term.

"The above account shows that Redureau has no current mental disturbance. It also tends to establish that at the moment he committed the murders of which he is accused, he was not under the influence of a pathological mental condition. All the same, this point deserves closer examination.

"The number of victims, the manner in which the murderer attacked them, and the fury that guided his arm suggest a priori the notion of some kind of passing delirium, such as are sometimes experienced in latent epileptic states and, rarely, in some states of intoxication. But we cannot accept this possibility for the following reasons: Redureau never displayed the slightest symptom of epilepsy. He wasn't under the influence of any intoxication or delirious disturbance but rather benefited from his full intelligence and maintained a complete awareness of all his actions during the fatal night—whereas amnesia is the pathognomonic symptom of temporary delirium, and a person having acted in a state of epileptic or epileptoid mental disturbance would not have retained any memory of the deeds done or at most would have retained just a few vague and confused elements.

"The testimony of the witness Ch—— stating that the accused had, two and a half months before the crime, expressed the notion that 'his employers should be killed,' introduced, from a psychiatric point of view, a new hypothesis: had Redureau long been haunted by a maniacal idea to kill his employer? Had he succumbed to an irresistible impulse to murder, as in some cases known to science?

"But first, Redureau denies the statement. Second, we've seen that he was never haunted by an idée fixe of any kind, and he always denied whatever we proposed on this point. In any case, the statement attributed to Redureau would be unlikely coming from a maniac. A person tormented by the impulse to murder suffers morally from this obsession: if he reproaches anyone, it is not his future victim but himself: he accuses himself instead of condemning someone else. Therefore, Redureau did not succumb to an obsession, nor did he obey an irresistible unconscious impulse.

"We tried to discover the accused's physical condition at the moment of the crime. Was he overworked, tired, or in a state of lesser organic or nervous resistance? Harvesting grapes is hard work, and we know, from a inquiry made at our request, that at Mabit's the day started at five o'clock in the morning and did not finish until ten in the evening, with no breaks apart from meals. But this inquiry also revealed that the grape harvest had been done in several stages separated by pauses for rest. They took place on the following dates in September: the seventeenth, eighteenth, and nineteenth; pause on the twentieth, twenty-first, and twenty-second, resuming from the twenty-third to the twenty-seventh. Sunday the twenty-eighth was a day of rest. They worked only part of the day on the twenty-ninth and all day long on the thirtieth, the day of the crime. As a result, the job, even though arduous for a fifteen-year-old, was interrupted on several occasions and was not carried out in conditions that would have resulted in physical overwork and real nervous exhaustion.[16]

"During our expert reports, the examining magistrate received and passed along to us an anonymous letter calling his attention to the disturbing effect of 'wine vapors in the wine presses where it is made and bottled' on the brains of men who work at this trade. Even though we had no medical reason to think that this cause could have been involved in Redureau's crime, we proceeded to make inquiries with competent medical authorities but received only negative reactions. None of the doctors consulted had observed any cerebral excitement that could be attributed to wine vapors. Indeed, let it be noted that there is far more stupefying gas than stimulating vapor let off by the must during fermentation. Carbonic gases predominate, and their properties cause asphyxiation rather than insane drunkenness.

16. Nevertheless, the defense attorney, Monsieur Durand, pointed out: "The experts say that the grape harvest was done in several stages separated by pauses for rest. That's true. But which pauses? If we take the dates cited by the experts and furnished by Monsieur Mabit, the victim's brother, here's what we observe:

"The grape harvest began on Wednesday of the third week of September. Three days were devoted to it that week: Wednesday, Thursday, and Friday, or September 17, 18, and 19. Then there was an interruption of a few days, but the following week, work began again on Tuesday and lasted through Saturday, inclusive. Sunday was observed as a day of rest, and on Monday afternoon they returned to harvesting. On Tuesday, September 30, from five o'clock in morning, the servant was at work with his master, and he was still there at 10:30 that night.

"How long did the work day last?

"Work started in the Mabit home at five o'clock in the morning. There were pauses only for meals. It finished at the earliest at ten o'clock at night."

. . . .

"By law, a workday for children of his age in an industrial firm must not exceed ten hours. But his days were fourteen and fifteen hours long.

"I'm not accusing Mabit of having been an inhuman master; at home he adopted the customs of the region where he lived. He imposed them on himself. But we must be totally candid here: he could have imposed them on day laborers who were from twenty-five to thirty years old; he was committing an error when he imposed the same system on a servant who was fifteen years old. Hence, I am not contradicting the experts in their recent statement, given with the authority that they possess, that the grape-harvest work did not create a condition of nervous exhaustion in the accused. But when afterward I read in their report that the explanation of the acts committed by Redureau must be sought in an especially irritable state of mind, then overwork clearly seems to me one of the causes that brought this irritability to an acute state."

"In any event, with reference to Redureau, it's established that since the start of the grape harvest, he spent the major part of his days in the open air, among the vines; work with the winepress took only a few hours each day, and on the night of the crime, he spent less than ninety minutes in the storeroom. He himself was very definite about the point that he was neither disturbed, excited, nor drunk when he stabbed his employer.

"In sum, the true determinants of the acts committed by the accused must be sought in normal adolescent psychology rather than in psychopathology. It is a standard idea that the developmental stage of puberty is marked by profound changes, not just in organic functions, but in psychic functions as well: sensitivity, intelligence, and willful activities. Just as physical resistance declines and the body offers less immunity against morbid influences, a kind of momentary break in mental balance occurs with the excessive development of an awareness of personality, exaggerated touchiness, and psychic hyperaesthesia. A real inclination to pugnacity is visible, as are a noteworthy exaggeration of impulsiveness and tendencies toward violence. The adolescent is very sensitive to praise and, by contrast, feels much more acutely any wounds to self-esteem. The impressions that arrive to his brain are more irresistibly changed into driving incitements or, in other words, impulsive acts. Specialists who work on pubescent psychology have noticed both that in schools the largest number of cases of subjects liable for punishment for bad behavior, disputes, and assault and battery occur in the fifteenth year, because on reaching that age, young people have minimal control of their primary impulses, and that thoughtlessness is the main attribute of their mental condition. Modern science finds this way of thinking to be the main cause of a predisposition to criminality in adolescents at the stage of puberty.

"The preceding allows us to understand the degree of violence to which certain impassioned impulses of adolescence may attain and how one must avoid applying to their interpretation any criterion drawn from the mentality of adults.

"Thus normally, certain acts that are difficult to explain, such as those of which the defendant is accused, may result from a mental condition that is in no way identifiable as pathology, that is, in a word, physiological. Let's add that Redureau, without being a degenerate from a psychic point of view, inarguably possesses a nervous temperament, and it seems established from diverse testimony that he has a particular personality termed 'shifty,' which doubtless might also be described by the words 'touchy and vindictive'; circumstances that certainly promoted within him an explosion of impulsiveness and violence.

"As a result, we are replying as follows to the questions that have been presented to us:

"1. Redureau, Marcel, was not in a state of dementia in the sense of article 64 of the penal code when he committed the acts of which he is accused.

"2. At the moment of the crime, he enjoyed normal judgment and full awareness of his actions.

"3. Psychiatric and biological examination did not reveal any mental or psychic anomaly. The observed characteristics of his temperament and personality remain within the limits of individual psychological variations and seem not of a nature to modify his responsibility."

Nantes, January 17, 1914

4

The defense lawyer's task was made especially difficult by this remarkable medical report, which almost necessitated the maximum penalty for Redureau. Despite the lawyer Durand's very fine defense speech, of which I will later quote some excerpts, his client was sentenced to twenty years' imprisonment.

It's rather disconcerting to think that in the current state of jurisprudence, it would have been better for the accused to have shown the signs of degeneracy typical of a person destined to commit a crime. A lack of responsibility, recognized by the doctors in this case, would have allowed the jurors to grant the benefit of "extenuating circumstances"; for Redureau, this would have meant a substantial reduction in his sentence. Faced with precise questions that required yes-or-no answers, the jurors were forced to reply in the affirmative; as they did, so would I have done. Once again I reflected that society is not protected, nor is our need for justice ideally satisfied, by such a trial. Nor should less draconian laws favor a predestined wrongdoer who has no choice but to kill over someone accidentally stricken by a "dementia brevis." I will stop here, because there would be too much to say about this question. But some might be grateful to see the following thoughts reproduced here, which I have taken from the speech of Monsieur Durand, the defense attorney, along with some of the quotations from eminent judges that he used during his summation. These honest reflections might sadly appear as mere quibbling to the far-too-often uneducated minds of most jurors. Jury selection, as we know, is left up to chance, and if, as Descartes claims, "good sense is the most evenly distributed thing in the world,"[17] we would never know it, alas, from the deliberations of a jury.

Nothing proves the defectiveness of a process whose absurdity I denounced in my *Memoir of the Assize Court* (an absurdity that has been observed many times since) better than the few lines that follow. It will be seen that to satisfy his feeling for justice, the juror has no choice but to say no, despite all the evidence, and that often forces him to say yes, in contradiction to all sense of justice.

First, let's observe the defense attorney's attempt to widen the noose of the medical report:

"The observed characteristics of his temperament and personality remain within the limits of individual psychological variations and seem to us not of a nature to modify his responsibility."

Monsieur Durand replied:

"I accept the first part of the opinion as expressed by the experts. The psychiatric and biological examinations did not reveal any mental or psychic anomaly. But I dispute the conclusion. It contradicts the thesis that has been developed on pubescent psychology. If I compare this thesis to the general principles of penal law, I am forcibly led to conclude that Redureau cannot be considered fully responsible for his acts."

Later Monsieur Durand added:

"The moral value of an act depends on the degree of freedom of the person who did it."

17. Tr. note: The philosopher René Descartes's *Discourse on the Method* (1637), pt. 1, begins with the ironic observation that "good sense is the most evenly distributed thing in the world, for all people think themselves so well provided with it that even those who are the most difficult to please in every other respect never seem to want more than they have."

And he quoted these words of Edmond Villey:

"'Freedom is the condition and justification for man's responsibility. By this we do not mean the physical possibility of acting in one way or another; animals have that kind of freedom, and we don't think of holding them accountable for their actions. We mean an intelligent and reasoned freedom. This means that two conditions form the basis for penal impunity; *intelligence,* in the sense of *moral reason,* which gives an idea of good and evil; and *free will* or *freedom,* which permits the choice between good and evil.' For his part, Professor Saleilles has written, 'Without freedom, no responsibility'; defining what he meant by freedom, he stated: 'Freedom is a condition, man's condition when in complete control of himself.'[18] Man is not responsible when he is in a state of madness; then he lacks both intelligence and freedom. Hence there is no crime or misdemeanor, according to article 64 of the penal code. The 1810 code did not accept that there could be irresponsibility apart from cases of mental illness and what medicine calls pathological conditions. But penal law has advanced since then, and the code itself has been transformed. It has emerged from its narrow conceptions. Gentlemen, the juries that have preceded you delivered verdicts that forced the legislative powers to temper the rigors of the code. The 1810 penal code did not admit any diminished responsibility apart from insanity. There was no taking into account extenuating circumstances. Even so, a jury often faced a man whose defense consisted of laying bare the circumstances of his life, all the inducements he experienced, and all the panic that may have blinded him; the jury would understand that even without madness, there might be different degrees of freedom. Unable to somehow calibrate the measure of responsibility, they would return a pure and simple acquittal. That's when lawmakers, on two consecutive occasions in 1824 and 1832, yielded to the jury's inclination and introduced extenuating circumstances. 'Judicial proof,' wrote

18. Tr. note: Raymond Saleilles (1855–1912), a professor at the Université de Paris, wrote *L'Individualisation de la peine; étude de criminalité sociale.* First published in 1911, this is a landmark text on French penal law, discussing the penal codes of 1791 and 1810. It has been translated by Rachel S. Jastrow as *The Individualization of Punishment* (Montclair, N.J.: Patterson Smith, 1968). Edmond-Louis Villey-Desmeserets (b. 1848), known as Edmond Villey, authored the influential *Précis d'un cours de droit criminel,* a landmark in the French bibliography of criminal law.

Saleilles, whose account I have just borrowed almost word for word, 'judicial proof must henceforth be based not only on conditions of pathological diagnostic, which is a relatively simple question of pure medical verification, but on the question of moral psychology, the question of knowing whether the (concrete) act was done in a condition of moral freedom.'"

Later on, trying to inform jurors about the consequences that their responses could have for the accused, Monsieur Durand told them the following, which motivated my preceding thoughts:

"Independent of the special question of judgment, to which I will return shortly, there will be two questions before you, gentlemen, about each of the seven victims: 'Did Redureau voluntarily kill them? . . .' You will reply yes. The subordinate question deals with aggravating circumstances. It will not be the same in the case of Mabit and the six others.

"The aggravating circumstance mentioned in the father's case is as follows: 'Did the homicide precede, accompany, or follow other crimes . . . ?'

"I ask you, gentlemen, to answer no to this question, and here's why: it's materially true that Mabit's murder accompanied, and preceded, the murder of the six other victims. But this purely material circumstance is insufficient to constitute aggravation as defined by law. The legislators wished to address moral simultaneity, whether a crime was perpetrated to make it easier to commit a further crime. For aggravating circumstances to exist, two crimes must have been planned as part of the same project. That's what our illustrious compatriot Faustin Hélie writes in his *Theory of the Penal Code* (vol. 3, no. 13047):[19] 'Generally,' he explains, 'two crimes may be considered as simultaneous only when they are committed as part of the same plan, the results of the same action, and are committed at the same time in the same place.' But it is quite certain that at the moment he struck Mabit, Redureau was not thinking about killing any other victims.

"You will therefore answer no to the subordinate question."

That's what the jurors entirely failed to do.

19. Tr. note: Faustin Hélie (1799–1884) was a French legal expert.

5

Finally, as a form of conclusion, let me quote the following appendix to the medical report:

"After two sessions that shed no new light on the trial, the jury rendered a guilty verdict on all charges, and the court gave Redureau the maximum sentence for his age, or *twenty years' imprisonment*.

"During the lawyers' summations, he was slumped on his bench, his head down and face tearful, looking like a naughty child who expects a severe punishment. Only the testimony of the witness Ch——, which tended to establish premeditation, provoked new and forceful denials from him.[20] He wept when his uncle appeared at the bar to testify. He also shed a few tears during the prosecution address and during his lawyer's speech for the defense. He was certainly no longer the precocious protagonist seen in the assize court.

"During Redureau's months of committal for trial, spent at the Nantes prison infirmary, he caused no noteworthy comment. The prison's chief warden offered testimony that was reported in the newspaper *Le Phare*: 'The witness remarked that Redureau is secretive, crafty, on his guard, and answers only in monosyllables. He sleeps well and eats well; he does not seem to be frightened by his trial. Whether the accused regretted his act he could not say, but Redureau did weep once after seeing his lawyer, he asserted' Redureau had not wept just once. He wept when he received a visit from his mother; he wept many times in front of us, when we evoked the memory of his victims. The day after his sentencing, he wept for a long time, crying bitterly as a child might; once his tears were dried, one could see him slowly returning to the changeability of feelings and lack of concern of a child, amused by everything, who laughs at a trifle and is fully open to the outside world's influences. Only the recollection of his family brought him back to reality for a moment and drew tears from him. On this subject, thanks to the kind help of Monsieur Abel Durand, the distinguished lawyer

---

20. It is noteworthy that at the session, the lawyer mentioned some evidence that tended to show the witness as a quasi-pathological liar (that's what we've been pointing out at some length).

in charge of his defense, we may offer a copy of the letter that he wrote to his parents the day after the verdict, a letter is highly chracteristic:

Dear Parents,

I am writing to tell you that the big day is over, but unfortunately without good results and as you must have already heard, I am sentenced to twenty long years of imprisonment in a penitentiary colony and as you see dear parents death will come to take us before we see one another again thats why you have to come to get my belongings because they will be lost and when you come do come on Saturday and Tuesday because the other days it is forbidden to see the prisoners other than on Tuesday and Saturday.

You won't forget to give me your address when you leave the place where we were doing so well before the evil day of September 30 when I committed the horrible crime that is keeping me away forever from such a good father and a good mother and such good brothers and sisters that I will never see again and my poor grand father who loved me so much I will never see him again and Clémentine and Bertha who I loved so much and Jean who is in Algiers who was so good to me what a shame for you all who have nothing to do with it. You will let me know if Marie is still at T—— because her friends must speak to her about me if she is still there and they must not look at her any more even though it is not her fault.

I have just learned from my lawyer that papa is very sick after leaving town I hope he will soon be cured by leaving this place of misfortune that was so fine before the crime by the miserable young man that I am.

I do not think I will stay at Nantes for long when I am moved to another spot I will give you the address so that I can receive your news because it would be too hard not to get any of it. When you answer me tell me the news of my dear father who is weeping for his son who is sentenced to never see him again, I think that he will be cured soon and that he will be brave and you will tell me the news of grandfather who must look older.

Your son who thinks about what he has done and who weeps when he thinks of such a horrible crime that gave you pain and shame for the rest of your life as well as that of my good brothers and sisters who will always weep over such a bad crime done by their young brother prisoner forever.

Your son who as he weeps kisses his good parents who are forever and always far away from him.

Marcel Redureau.[21]

---

21. We have not corrected the spelling or punctuation.

"In its mixture of naive concern and apparently sincere regret, this letter forms a psychological document that seems to fully confirm our judgment of its young author's mind and needs no further comment."

⚘ ⚘ ⚘

"After the sentencing," writes Monsieur Gaëtan Rondeau, my kind correspondent, "Marcel Redureau's contact with his lawyer continued. The latter remained perplexed by the psychological mystery, whose secret will doubtless not be revealed by in-depth study of the case. After the verdict and until his death, Marcel Redureau displayed exemplary emotions, and until the end, his defender could not help but feel sympathy for him somewhat analogous to that felt by Mauriac for his 'criminal' protagonists.[22] Marcel Redureau died of tuberculosis in the X—— correctional colony around February 1916. A few weeks earlier his defense attorney had received a touching letter of farewell from him. His conduct at the colony was always satisfactory."

22. Tr. note: The French Catholic author François Mauriac (1885–1970) wrote novels that featured villainous characters, such as the miser Louis in *Noeud de vipères* (Knot of vipers; 1932) or Gradere in *Les Anges noirs* (The dark angels; 1936). In 1959, when Mauriac criticized the gay novelist Roger Peyrefitte, Peyrefitte responded by "outing" Mauriac. Gide's relations with Mauriac were difficult as well.

⚘ ⚘ ⚘ News Items

First Letter about News Items

Quite a long time ago I received, from an unknown correspondent, the following amusing letter in response to my first article of *News Items,* published in the *N.R.F.:*

Paris, February 7, 1927

Sir,

    You're looking for news items that force us to think. None has ever interested me more, in fact, than the following: that the man generally called the shrewdest critic of our era, whom I myself consider the most expert and least "gullible," should allow himself to hope that an audience will grasp the interest of news items in the same way that he does, to expect of unknown persons that these anecdotes will overturn within them the same too easily accepted ideas that they overturn within him, as if everyone felt the same joy at seeing his prejudices toppled and as if the same prejudices, with the same degree of criticism, is found in others, equally ready to be toppled. How can you attribute to others the reforming virtues about which you write? Moreover, have you anticipated what it is about the unknown that fascinates you, and have you a precise idea of what to expect?

    Yet, am I not in fact answering your request? The request and the disappointment that you admit to are in themselves the news item that you describe: mysterious, contradicting opinions that I had previously formed, evocative, and troubling.

But if I've succeeded, it's with the impression of thinking in a way that is contrary to your own thought. Is that what you wanted? I myself remain unsatisfied, but I enjoy seeing that you, André Gide, wish to communicate the restlessness of your mind to different minds, annexing them to think through them, to make this pan-Gideism widen your own field of investigation.

. . . .

Max Terrier[1]

There is certainly much truth in this letter. I didn't publish it immediately for fear of discouraging other correspondents. But I think it's time to admit it now: basically, I don't believe much in "news items." Doubtless they can be highly evocative; many of them would be, if only one could see them closely enough. But at least such as they are presented by newspapers, they are most often so insignificant that weeks and months go by without my discovering a single one that seems worthy of attention.

Newspapers all present the same ones, and nearly in the same manner. No doubt an agency provides them a text, which they merely reproduce. When they add their own invention to it, what occurs? This other letter, from July 10, 1927, with an illegible signature, offers an answer:

Saint-Blain, July 10th

Sir,

Allow me to send you a "news item" that may perhaps interest you even more for its context than for itself. Here it is:

Twelve-Year-Old Girl Criminal.

In Bari (Italy) a twelve-year-old girl met a little three-year-old girl who was lost and looking for her parents. Moved by a spirit of wickedness, she

---

1. Tr. note: The French historian Max Terrier (1902–?) coedited *1848* (Paris: Tel Quel, 1948).

*took the little girl by the hand, led her to an isolated place, and threw her
into a well, in which the little one drowned.*[2]

(Feuille d'avis de Neuchâtel, July 7, 1927)

Once the information was gathered, the news was conveyed
to the paper by the Agence Télégraphique Suisse. I phoned their
office, and this is what I learned:

The Agence Télégraphique Suisse itself had received the news
from an Italian agency that had sent it along *without the words
"moved by a spirit of wickedness."* After I expressed surprise at
this addition, I was told: "People are not normally killed that
way . . . , even at that age. . . . All we did was to add *the only
plausible explanation.*"

Therefore these folk don't accept miracles, for it would be a
miracle for them, and the very meaning of a miracle, although

2. To be compared with another news item that many newspapers have printed using the
same terms (see especially *Le Temps,* September 9, 1927):

"The crime of a fifteen-year-old child.—Last August 31, the disappearance of a little girl
aged six, Jeanne Mullier, was announced. After several days of fruitless searching, the child's
corpse was finally found in the well of an abandoned quarry near her home. The police have
arrested the murderer, a fifteen-year-old boy, Florimond Robitaillie, whose house is near little
Jeanne's. Questioned all yesterday and last night, he made a full confession at 2 A.M. He gave
the following account of his crime:

"'I made a date to meet Jeanne in the tunnels. We had some fun there, but she fell and hurt
herself, and I was afraid she would tell her parents everything, and I led her where it was dark,
toward the well, where I knew she would fall in. She did slip into the water, in fact, and I
watched her die by the light from my flashlight. It took ten minutes. When I saw that she was
dead, I went back up again, and afterward I was working as if nothing had happened.'"

I confess that I'm slightly dubious about the phrase "I was afraid she would tell her parents everything." Was this truly spoken by the child? Or is it rather like "moved by a spirit of
wickedness," artificially provoked by an interrogation or added by a journalist (or news
agency) wishing to present a rational explanation of an item that, I daresay, itself is irrational; an explanation as likely to falsify meaning as were the often involuntary interpretations,
of which Lévy-Bruhl rightly complains, of the facts he reported during his research for *The
Primitive Mentality,* based on stories by missionaries and explorers. [Tr. note: Lucien Lévy-
Bruhl (1857–1939) was an eminent French social scientist. In *La Mentalité primitive* (1922)
Lévy-Bruhl includes anecdotes suggesting that what is experienced in dreams is authentic
and as important as waking experiences.] But both concede our mind's irresistible need to
explain and classify facts that are incomprehensible—in the present state of psychological
science, and certainly deeply disconcerting—according to the banal ideas of accepted rudimentary psychology.

reborn among some people, has died out for most of our contemporaries; a gratuitous act is out of the question.

At the very idea of it, these people are so disturbed that they add what seems to them to be an explanation, and what's more, a cause . . . wickedness . . . "spirit of wickedness," that's the logical label.

A gratuitous act . . . Let's be clear. Personally I don't believe in gratuitous acts, an act without any motivation. That is fundamentally out of the question. There are no effects without causes. The words "gratuitous act" are a *temporary* label that seems convenient to describe acts that transcend ordinary psychological explanations, gestures that do not result in simple personal advantage (in this way I might speak of *disinterested* acts, with a slight play on words).[3] Nevertheless, let's reiterate: man acts either to obtain . . . something, or *with something in mind,* or simply from internal motivation. In the same way, someone who is walking may head toward something or simply advance without any purpose other than to make progress, to "push ahead." In the first case, if a judge asks such people, Why did you do that? they may give a reason (good or bad). Those in the second group can reply only, Because I felt like doing it. (Needless to say, many from the first group would give the same answer if they were perfectly sincere or perceptive.) All this is elementary. I have described, in my *Memoir of the Assize Court,* a judge's extreme confusion and incomprehension when faced with this sort of act—I mean a "disinterested" act. The case in question was a young arsonist who clearly (at least to my eyes, as a juror) set fires purely for pleasure, out of a simple need to burn, giving in to a naive and urgent impulse, an imperious impulse (we are free to try to analyze and deconstruct it later); certain replies from the accused led me to suppose that an erotic aspect entered into the arson, a sexual perversion, and that it can be suitably regarded as a special type of sadism. The buildings set afire by the arsonist belonged to his own family; thus, indirectly, he was bankrupting himself.

3. Tr. note: Gide puns here on *actes désintéressés* (disinterested or selfless acts) and *actes des intéressés* (i.e., acts by selfish or self-seeking people).

"Then why did you do it?" the president stubbornly inquired. "Hate? Jealousy? Envy?"

The man could only reply, "I did it because I felt like doing it."

"At least admit that you were drunk."

"No. I didn't drink anything that day."

The president put his hands to his head and gave up trying to understand. Yes, Your Honor, give up; cede your place to a doctor.

And confronted by certain cases—especially that of young Redureau—even the pathologist is perplexed.

Second Letter about News Items

Alas, I am forced to admit that most of the fairly numerous letters that I have received in response to the article about news items have disappointed me. Most of my new correspondents don't even seem to understand the kind of special interest that we have a right to expect from a "news item."

Why should I care, for example, that to get rid of an old man, a poisoner used a dose of arsenic capable of exterminating six people? Only puerilities can be found therein, along with the silliness of some reporters and the accommodations they make for some readers. But what do I care for the picturesque, macabre, or "sensational"?

Neither vain curiosity nor the desire to amuse readers made me create this column. I feel that psychology (not that of philosophers, if you please) of the sort "in daily use" is based on commonplaces and poorly controlled data, and its decisions are often distorted. I perceive a great deal of laziness and scant critical spirit. Unfortunately, most novelists and playwrights are satisfied with banal and dubious data that authorizes facile effects and guarantees public approval. It is a paper currency with a daily rate, whose true cash reserves do not guarantee its value; it's a merely conventional value.

I am interested in news items that jar any too easily accepted ideas, forcing us to think.

Nothing can shed light on my thoughts better than a letter that I read in *La Presse médicale* (November 1926),[4] the importance of which will be grasped by the readers of the *N.R.F.* I am quoting it without further personal comment. Let each one draw from it the conclusions that he may wish.

Russian Suicides during the Revolution.

Doctor Suzanne Serin has just published in *La Presse médicale* of November 6, 1926, a substantial medico-social investigation of 307 suicides, those resulting in death as well as attempts. According to her, "destitution is a great purveyor of suicides." Indeed: 38 cases out of 307.

Now, if ever there were an immense and tragic field open to a "medico-social" investigation of suicide, none can equal the Russian Revolution and subsequent famine.

A priori, a dreadful rash of psychic disturbances might be predicted, along with a rising number of suicides.

I was well situated to see the tragedy unfold, as I have practiced medicine in Saint Petersburg since 1901, treating patients on all social levels.

Every day, there was a *Suicides* column in the newspapers. There I noted that the number was from five to twenty per day and per city. Everyone around us had friends who had committed suicide: psychosis? melancholy? poverty? Most often, we decided, "poverty." An odd poverty indeed in a land and a time when a pound of bread cost only five centimes and a pound of meat was fifty centimes, a land where free soup kitchens were capable of feeding all the poor.

In 1917 the tempest was unleashed, followed immediately by famine. But contrary to all predictions, the amount of psychosis did not grow, and amazingly enough, *people no longer committed suicide.* They had lots of other things to do . . . for, forced into the most atrocious, prolonged famine, they had to find a way to live on a thousand calories per day and accustom their organisms to this permanent malnutrition.

But when the body is cleaned out and lightened to this extent, only one instinct remains, vast, unbounded—*not to die of hunger!* . . .

When the terrific life instinct gets to work, there is no more room for suicide.

Marcou-Mutzner (Ajaccio),
Former Intern, Paris Hospital System.

4. I especially thank Dr. J. Bercher, who sent it to me.

⚜ ⚜ ⚜

To encourage my correspondents, I didn't limit myself to news items printed in newspapers. I didn't dare ask for personal stories, out of a real fear of being deluged and already receiving far too many "secrets." But in another domain that is still directly linked with psychology, here is what I suggest (as an example):

Curiosity is one of the motives for our activity that seems to be the most misunderstood and least well studied. In vain do I scour psychology treatises for any mention of it. William James ignores the question, which nonetheless seems to me to be among the most important ones. It seems to me that curiosity exists in a more-or-less rudimentary form in animals. Until now I have not managed, perhaps for want of sufficient data, to explain it clearly to myself or to be satisfied with the explanation offered by a certain philosopher, with whom I discussed it. If my cat sees that a cupboard door is ajar, he won't rest until he's gone inside it.—He hopes to find something to satisfy his appetite.—More than that. He's just eaten and isn't hungry any more. He's quite simply looking to see what is inside. It's precisely this "quite simply" that irritates me and that I find to be not at all simple. Does he *imagine* something? Should my question be absorbed in another: what is the role of imagination in animals? They are not all equally curious. Dogs seem to me to be very rarely that way (and perhaps carnivores in general), monkeys are (I believe) excessively curious, and what of curiosity among ruminants, which seems difficult to explain, given their form of nourishment? In the courtyard of the caïd of Tozeur,[5] where we slept, two half-tamed little gazelles live. If we opened our valise, they inevitably approached, curiosity triumphing over their shyness, clearly wanting to see what was inside. And without looking so far away, why do cows look at a passing train? How to explain what motivates them, to follow a passerby all along the fence of an enclosure and run to the other side of a field to better see him? If some observations might be made, liable, if not to resolve, at least to shed some light on my question, I would be grateful if they could be sent to me.

5. Tr. note: Tozeur is an oasis city in southwestern Tunisia, near the chott el Djerid, 450 kilometers southwest of the city of Tunis. Gide described his Tunisian travels in his book *Amyntas*.

Unfortunately, requests of the kind that I am making here most often remain unanswered. Is their importance not understood? A number of years ago (it was before the war), in an *N.R.F.* column, I reported certain observations that I was able to make about the habits of finches. I noted that in Normandy, during nesting season, certain finch households consisted of two males for every female. The fact seemed to me so strange that at first I doubted my observation, but I could see, during a visit I made to Arco, that once again finches were forming a household of three. When I expressed surprise to the bellboy to see two males, plus a female, busy feeding a single brood, the boy told me, "Yes, that lady finch has two husbands." The testimony of a bellboy did not satisfy me. I wanted confirmation. I appealed to the readers of the *N.R.F.* At the time there were fewer of them. I received no letters at all. Will I be more successful this time?

How few people there are who have a taste for observation and also know how to observe. An unbiased mind, inclined to criticism, is needed. Most often people see without looking and, based on what they see, draw rash conclusions in the manner of the natives of Gabon, who are described in this story that I have excerpted from a travel account:

"We must have been traveling for an hour. The songs of the paddlers and the steady swaying of the boat had gently put me to sleep. Suddenly a collision was felt. We had run aground on a tree trunk hidden under the water. Fortunately, it didn't make a hole in the bottom of the pirogue, but it was impossible to get free. It swiveled on its hull without moving forward.

"After a long wait, the natives from a neighboring village came to our aid and started to unload the pirogue. Monsieur E—— was carried away in their boat, with no result. Then came the turns of Monsieur C—— and Monsieur O——, still without any result. But as soon as I was taken from the pirogue, it floated again. "He's the father of all heaviness!" shouted the natives; "he's the one we should have started with!"

1. Suicides in Russia from 1918 to 1923

I'm pleased to offer our readers an appendix to the preceding letter in the form of this letter from Monsieur G. Mequet, whom I heartily thank:

Sir,

I read in the *N.R.F.* of February 1 a letter reprinted from *La Presse médicale* of November 1926 about suicides in Russia.

In it, Doctor M. M. points to a decline in the number of suicides after the revolution and attributes this fact to a sort of frenzy in the struggle against poverty.

I shall allow myself to make a few observations on this subject based on two charts that I excerpt from the *Collection of U.S.S.R. Statistics* for the period of 1918–1923 (p. 82).

(a) The decline in the *total* number of suicides is very perceptible after 1914.

In Moscow the total number of suicides fell from 360 in 1913 to 172 in 1916. During the revolutionary period, it fell from 127 in 1917 to 64 in 1920, only to increase in 1921 (a year of famine) to 98 and 220 in 1922.

In Petrograd it fell from 588 in 1913 to 267 in 1916, then to 241 in 1917 and 183 in 1920, climbing to 183 in 1921 and 286 in 1922.

There we have the total number of suicides, confirming more or less the personal observations of Dr. M. M.

To be more exact, we must take into account the fact that the population of the large cities varied widely during this period. Petrograd's population fell from 2,100,000 to 700,000 inhabitants.

When we consult the second chart, which gives the proportion of suicides per million inhabitants, we observe rather different changes.

In Moscow the annual average in 1914–16 was 207; in 1917, 137; in 1920, 125; in 1921, 191; in 1922, 431.

In Petrograd, in 1914, 211; in 1917, 105; thus a strong decline, but the number went up again starting in 1919 with 237; in 1920, 546; in 1921, 568; and in 1922, 877.

(b) The two charts show clearly that *men* did not stop committing suicide. Yet it's extremely curious that the proportion of women among the suicides augmented from 30 percent in 1914 to 45 percent in 1920 in Moscow. In Petrograd the proportion reached 42 percent in 1920 and 47 percent in 1921.

(c) It's possible that poverty, beyond certain limits, takes away even the strength necessary to commit suicide. Yet this explanation seems insufficient for the Russian situation.

There is no doubt that the total and relative numbers of suicides (I note that I've forgotten to indicate that the statistics I am quoting mention only cases of suicide with a fatal result, not including mere suicide attempts) have declined, but the number of suicidable persons—if I may venture a macabre adjective—seems to have considerably declined also. Poor people from large cities were in the army during the war, to a large degree; others, above all women and children, easily found adequate salaries in the war industry.

And during the civil war, one might ask? There was still the army—whether red or white—and many modest folk fled to participate in the division of the land. Finally, poor people may have had more reason for hope at the time than did people of the dispossessed classes.

(d) Doctor M. M.'s remark about the influence of poverty deserves to be discussed again, in depth. More detailed statistics allow us to observe a strong increase in the proportion of young people and children among the suicides. Finally, what is even more striking, suicides among the population of illiterates were comparatively few.

Monsieur G. Mequet,
5, avenue Ernest Pictet, Geneva

2. The "Epidemic of Suicides" in America

Several Parisian newspapers have reprinted this dispatch:

A Club against Suicide

Baltimore, March 2.

Alarmed by the epidemic of suicides that is currently wreaking havoc among students in the United States, a club to check the progress of this contagion has been organized at the University of Baltimore. The thirteen young people who have assumed leadership of the club plan to study the reasons that have driven their friends to kill themselves. Once they know the motives for these desperate acts, they will find a means to prevent any future repetition of such crimes.[6]

Let's hope so.

3. Suicides

1. *A desperate man poisons himself and describes the last minutes of his life in a letter.*

"Last Saturday, having lunched as usual at eleven o'clock, the head clerk in a bookstore in Luton, a small city in Sussex, returned to the store where his employer, Mr. Thomas Edward Maw, awaited him. Great was the young man's surprise to find the bookseller collapsed over a table, apparently asleep. His surprise changed to horror when he observed that the old man, whom he had left a half-hour before, joyous and perfectly healthy of body, was dead. A sheet of paper was spread out in front of the corpse. It was covered in writing, an even script that became oddly zigzagging and halting. The dead man held a pencil between his stiffened fingers. There was no longer any doubt: it was indeed he who had written this final letter, of which here are the contents:

"'11:05! My clerk has just left. I have taken a vial of potassium cyanide from a drawer. The hour of death has come. I will end this bad joke that is called life.

"'11:08! I swallow the contents of the vial. It doesn't taste bad. A few more seconds and it's over. A customer has come in. I dare not get up, for fear of collapsing at his feet. One must die as a gentleman. The first

6. Tr. note: Regarding this suicide epidemic, see Winifred Richmond, "Mental Hygiene in the Colleges," *Journal of the American Medical Association* 93 (December 21, 1929): 1936–39. From January to April 1927 American newspapers reported an "epidemic" of U.S. college student suicides, totaling twenty-six. By April, however, statisticians had denied that there was an epidemic. Nevertheless, to combat the supposed trend, by 1928 mental health programs had been launched at sixteen universities, including West Point, Dartmouth, Vassar, Harvard, and Yale. According to its Web site (www.ubalt.edu), the University of Baltimore was founded in 1925 as a private institution. Gide's clipping does not mention a year but is likely from 1927, so the University of Baltimore suicide club must have been formed shortly after the university itself was launched.

symptoms. Dizziness. My brain is throbbing horribly. A few more brief seconds, so brief.

"'11:12! Terror. It's coming. I'm afraid. I . . .'

"Destiny broke off the phrase, along with the life of the man who was writing it."

(*Le Soir de Bruxelles,* October 20, 1926)

2. A suicidal man jots down his last feelings.

"The war left Auguste Brunet, forty years old, living on boulevard Ornano in Paris, with an incurable malady. Life no longer offered him the least pleasure, and on Friday, exhausted, he resolved to die. After having copiously filled his stove with anthracite, he stretched out on his bed and, not wanting a banal suicide, began to describe his death throes in writing:

"'10:30: I'm starting to get a headache. 11:00: I'm breathing carbonic gas, but I still have all my faculties. 11:20: This is taking a long time.'

"Probably brought up on classical memoirs, and recalling the way that elegant men in imperial Rome could make a voluptuous death come quickly, he took a knife from his night table and opened veins on his wrists, and as his writing case became stained with blood, he continued to note down: 'My strength is ebbing away. I feel a gentle pleasure flooding inside me. 12:15: Death must be gentle, and my worthless tatters expect it without any fear. I hear singing. I too am joyful. 1P.M.: I've widened the openings through which my blood is flowing. The bells are chiming. May my little Marthe forgive m——'

"The sinister, gentle dream stops with an unfinished word. When the bloodless body was discovered, it looked as if it were resting tranquilly. The desperate man bequeathed his body to the Academy of Medicine."

(*Le Soir de Bruxelles,* April 20, 1927)

3. The suicide of a high-school student.

"We have noted the dramatic suicide of young Nény, barely fifteen years old, who in the middle of a class at the lycée Blaise Pascal, in Clermont-Ferrand, blew out his brains with a revolver shot.

"The *Journal des débats* has received the following odd information from Clermont-Ferrand:

"That a poor child, raised in a family where violent scenes occurred—including the night before his death—often obliging him to sleep at the neighbors' house, had been brought to the idea of suicide is a painful, although excusable, thing; that the constant unsupervised reading of pessimistic German philosophers led him into a worthless mysticism—'his own religion,' as he called it—may also be excused. But that in the secondary school of a large city a group of evil-minded youngsters should incite one another to suicide is unnatural, and sadly, that is what must be told.

"There was said to be a drawing of lots among three students to know who would be the first to kill himself. It is certain that the unfortunate Nény's two accomplices more or less forced him to do so, by accusing him of cowardice. The night before they had him perform a rehearsal and staging of the loathsome act. The spot where he would blow out his brains on the next day was marked on the ground with chalk. A young student entered at this moment and saw the rehearsal. He was thrown out by the three wrongdoers, with this threat: 'You know too much; you're going to disappear'—and it seems that there was a list of those who were going to disappear.

"It is certain that ten minutes before the final scene, a classmate sitting next to Nény borrowed a watch from another student and told Nény, 'You know that you must kill yourself at 3:20; you only have ten—five—two minutes left!'

"At the exact time the unfortunate boy stood up, went to the spot marked with chalk, pulled out a revolver, and shot himself in the right temple.

"It's also true that when he fell, one of the conspirators had the self-possession to throw himself on the revolver and make it disappear.

"It still has not been found. What will it be used for?

"All this is horrible, and the parents of students are extremely upset, which is understandable!"

(*Journal de Rouen,* June 5, 1909)

4. *The suicide of Count Hasnic.*

"Count Hasnic, of Polish origin, arrived in Paris possessing a great fortune. He lived in lavish style and after a few months found himself nearly bankrupt.[7]

"Then he returned to Poland, hoping to regain his riches, but he didn't succeed as he had hoped. In his homeland, however, he met a charming young woman whom he brought back with him when he returned to Paris.

"The count continued his life of luxury and gambling. The day before yesterday, he was in his usual haunt, on the boulevard des Capucines, when one of his friends who had maintained his own fortune entered. Count Hasnic proposed a game of écarté.[8] His friend accepted. The count won almost all the hands and found himself holding a relatively substantial sum, when another gambler who had just entered addressed the count's friend, saying:

"'But how are you playing, dear friend? You're discarding all the winning cards!'

"Count Hasnic, very pale, stood up immediately.

"'I understand,' he told his friend. 'Thanks, but I cannot accept.'

"And he went out.

"An hour later he killed himself with a revolver shot in a room he had just taken in a hotel near the gare Saint-Lazare"

(*Le Temps*, January 4, 1908)

7. Tr. note: According to the Polish social historian Wojciech Karpinski of the Centre National de la Recherche Scientifique, Paris, Hasnic is not a Polish name, and no Count Hasnic is known to have been a member of the Polish émigré community at the turn of the century (personal communication).

8. Tr. note: L'écarté is a card game with two players and a thirty-two-card deck that was popular in the mid-nineteenth century. It was often played for large sums in social settings or gambling parlors.

4. Scenes of Unanimism in Russia[9]

For Jules Romains

1. *The Doukhobors.*[10]

"More than forty-five Doukhobors, men, women, and children, took to the road to preach about the way to lead a healthy life. 'Starting on May 12,' Alexey Mukhortov wrote, 'we set out in the manner of Adam and Eve to demonstrate naturalness to humanity, how man must return to his nourishing mother, to ripe fruits and their seeds.

"'We stripped naked at Efremooka and finished our trip at Nadezhda. We went through a total of sixteen villages. We were stopped and set upon with switches. We were all bloody, frightful to see.

"'Then about twenty men surrounded us and did not allow us to enter the village. Night came, and the weather was awful, with rain, snow, wind. We piled up, one on top of another. Those who guarded us spent the night near us and covered us with lambskin cloaks and overcoats. We remained naked and yet, as amazing as it might seem in such a wind, none of us was frozen. Those who kept watch declared nevertheless that the cold was very bitter!'

"Reduced to twenty-eight, they appeared on May 21 at Yorkton, where the mounted police met them. 'We stopped,' he said, 'undressed, and advanced.' They were forced to put on their clothes again; the next day they were sentenced to three months in prison, which they served in Regina. They refused to submit to prison routine, considering, not without reason this time, that they had done nothing to merit the loss of their freedom. The Canadian jailers apparently acted toward them

9. Tr. note: Unanimism is a literary concept, advanced by Gide's friend the writer Jules Romains (1885–1972), describing a collective spirit considered as godly. Romains's 1905 article "Les Sentiments unanimes et la poésie" and poetry collection *La Vie unanime* (1908) expounded this brand of human pantheism focused on collectivity and groups, in which individuals are mystically linked with one another and with nature.

10. Tr. note: The Doukhobors were a Russian religious group whose name means "spirit wrestler." Founded in the century, the pacifist sect disdained all church tradition and ritual, which resulted in exile, beatings, and imprisonment. Supported by Leo Tolstoy and foreign groups, the Doukhobors migrated to Canada in 1899, and despite difficulties, some still live there.

with Cossack brutality. They were beaten with ropes and whips until their bodies were covered with bruises; their beards and hair were pulled, their wrists were wrenched, their heads were shoved into buckets, and they were held up by their heels until they choked. A certain Peter Zirtchoukof was struck with chairs until he fell down in a faint.

"When their prison sentences were over, they returned home. Of the twenty-eight, all but ten "retrogressed," that is to say, went back to their original work.

"'After waiting a little, we (the ten righteous men) began again to busy ourselves with God's work. We crushed wheat with a roller (on foot) over an area of fifty meters. Why? In order that man should not trust human science. . . . We also set fire to a trap. Why? So that our brothers would not torment unfortunate animals. We were going to set fire to a threshing machine but were prevented from doing so. Six of us were arrested and sent to Yorkton.

"'As for myself, I'm still here, since I was not present at the time of the fire. But I'm no longer permitted to visit the other villages. It's so sad that I can't even think about it. I sit down and remain here without "working." Humanity does not want my work, and yet it isn't *my* work; it's God's. I've spent a week in this hut, with the windows nailed shut, like a prison.'

"One should add that Verigin proved quite hostile to this movement that had no future.[11] It was even at his instigation, it seems, that the six arsonists were arrested and thrown into prison, handcuffed, as Mukhortov described; they were convicted on proof presented by the Doukhobors. Soon afterwards Verigin was told that a petition from the Doukhobors bearing his own seal might free them. Verigin rejected the proposal."

(From a letter by Alexey Mukhortov,
published in the *Svobodne Slovo* [Tolstoyan
newspaper] on September 29, 1903)

11. Tr. note: Peter Verigin (1859–1924), known as "Peter the Lordly," became the leader of the Doukhobors in Russia in 1887 and, after a lengthy Siberian exile, arrived in Canada in 1902, after organizing a mass migration of his group.

2. A village of widows in the U.S.S.R.

"In Russia, around the area of Novaia Laloga, is a village whose population seemed extraordinary to the district authorities, when they were told of it: it was a village of widows, in which not a single man remained out of the sixty-odd once known to live there. An investigation revealed that all the husbands had been murdered by their wives. There was a total of fifty-eight victims.

"The instigator of this massacre was a peasant woman named Sofia Safarina, who had killed her own three husbands. Their bodies, when exhumed, were found to contain traces of poison. Indeed, poison was the method all the village women used to get rid of their too-trusting husbands, whom they had first helped to get drunk.

"The housewives' crimes began just after the war. The brutal habits the men had brought back from the front, after a long period during which the women acted as they pleased, were said to have motivated the serial executions. Sofia Safarina, who alone had around thirty murders on her conscience, claimed to have been brought to 'androphobia' by the tyranny of her first husband."

(*La Croix,* September 30, 1927)

3. Fourteen Russians burn along with a church

"Berlin, July 2—From Moscow comes the following unbelievable news: the church of the small village of Kustanai was aflame, and firemen hurried to it. They found the doors solidly bolted and heard hymns being sung inside. The little church was completely burned, and the corpses of fourteen people were found in the ruins. They all are said to belong to a religious sect that considers Bolshevism as the reign of the Antichrist. The fourteen people discovered there no doubt considered that it was their duty to abandon a world that had become the kingdom of Satan."

(*Daily Mail,* July 5, 1927)

5. On the "Curiosity" of Animals

I have received a number of letters on the subject of curiosity. The most sensible, it seems to me, do not wish me to use the term *curiosity* when speaking of animals.

"Curiosity, requiring a certain intelligence, seems to me incompatible with a wholly instinctive animal. . . . animal curiosity is nothing other than stupor," writes Monsieur Albert Cornet. More scientifically, Monsieur A. L. Palan writes:

"What we call [he might have said: 'What you call'; I wouldn't have been offended] superficially *curiosity* in an animal is only the fulfillment of an inclination of biological origin. To explain certain animal movements by curiosity is to complicate the problem unnecessarily. To explain the same movements as the fulfillment of lower inclinations is to simplify it aptly. . . .

"What may we conclude? One soon notices that the problem of curiosity in animals does not exist, that it's a pseudo-problem. The animal does not seek what it imagines and supposes to exist (in other words, it doesn't imagine anything); . . . for it, there is no unknown but only either what is unimportant or unfamiliar."

Perfect. And I would apologize for having used this unsuitable word, if it hadn't in fact elicited these responses.

These reflections are confirmed by some examples sent by other correspondents and from what Christy informs me in his remarkable book *Big Game and Pygmies*,[12] from which I quoted several times in my account of a trip to equatorial Africa:

Goliaths, or enormous beetles, are fairly numerous in certain parts of the great Congolese forest; but they live in the tops of very high trees, and it would be very difficult to grab them, were they not irresistibly attracted to the unusual. The insect hunter who travels in these regions need only strew an open area in front of his hut with various groom-

---

12. Tr. note: Cuthbert Christy (1863–1932) was a British explorer and naturalist. His books include *Big Game and Pygmies; Experiences of a Naturalist in Central African Forests in Quest of the Okapi* (London: Macmillan, 1924). This account of game and game birds in Central Africa also contains information about the Mbuti people and the Ituri Forest. Christy also published *The African Rubber Industry and Funtumia Elastica* (London: J. Bale, Sons, and Danielsson, 1911).

ing or household objects, brushes, combs, and knives, preferably bright and shiny; the goliaths will fly toward these, landing on them or next to them, and one need only bend down to collect them.

Surely it would be absurd to speak of the *curiosity* of goliaths. The insects, one might say, are attracted by the splashes of color, as they doubtless would be by flowers—and, I also believe, in an even simpler manner, as larks are attracted by the traditional mirror. It is to be noted that this instinct leads the animal to its death, and I wonder if it isn't akin to the *fascination* that makes a bird hasten into a snake's gaping maw. I also believe that in this fascination may be seen the embryo of human curiosity. But this is taking us too far afield. Let's leave it for later.

Here is what my friend S. B. tells me:

"As a child I had no greater pleasure than to accompany a certain extraordinarily skilled birdcatcher into the woods. He built little traps for nightingales, which he baited and set at the foot of trees, on the moss, among dead leaves. But he didn't just set them. At first I was surprised to see him striking numerous and apparently quite useless little affected poses around the traps: 'That's just what attracts the nightingales,' he explained. 'It intrigues them, and they come to see what it is. However well placed a trap is, if I just set it, the nightingale won't come.' He caught lots of them."

⚘ ⚘ ⚘

Some letters reached me too late, and the observations they contain could not be included in my last article, dealing with curiosity in animals.

As an appendix to the article, I'm pleased to transcribe here some remarks from my friend J. P.:

"You recall what La Rochefoucauld said about curiosity (that it 'is not the love of novelty; but there is a selfish kind, that makes us want to take precedence in knowing things; and a proud kind, that makes us want to be above all those who are unaware of things and not to be beneath those who know do them.') Perhaps that's a little too simple, despite its scholarly appearance, but it's less overly simple than Monsieur Palan is. I suspect that what he calls 'the fulfillment of an inclination to a biological state' means simply an 'action' or 'movement.' The real question is what conscience, type of thought, and perhaps illusion accompanies a movement or 'fulfillment of the inclination,' etc. Any solution depends on the opinion that one has formed about animal thought. So be it. But this opinion does not contain any scientific rigor, and so it is slightly false to speak in this context of tendencies and biology.

"Anyway, the question of animal thought seems to me difficult and rather poorly presented. Perhaps we'd resolve it better if we started off with a lower opinion of human thought; if we noticed, for example, that metaphysicians might appear to angels, who (I suppose) do not know our language, to be men much like any others, only clumsier than most and less vigorous. These same signs in general define stupidity in animals.

"Let's return to La Rochefoucauld. Basically, he simply denies the existence of human curiosity, as Monsieur Palan does that of animals— but perhaps in a more ingenious way. Yet it's just this ingeniousness that makes him fail. For were his explanation true, it would become curiously inexplicable that there is no primary distinction made between proud and selfish curiosity and that we can even speak of curiosity as a simple feeling at all."

🙟 🙟 🙟

From a long and very interesting letter from Professor J. Strohl,[13] dean of the Faculty of Sciences at Zurich, I will excerpt without comment the following lines on the same subject:

"I recall having observed many times, during my childhood in Alsace, the curiosity of nightingales. When we heard this bird singing somewhere and wanted to see it, all we had to do was scratch the ground a bit near the place where it sang and hide ourselves nearby. The bird would quickly approach, to come and examine closely the inch of ground that had been disturbed. Isn't that the same instinct that attracts a bird to a bit of soil disturbed by an earthworm? . . .

13. Tr. note: Jean (Johannes) Strohl (1886–?) was a natural historian and author.

"Some analogous observations made about weasels kept in captivity led me to another assumption. Once returned after having been removed for a moment from their master's library, of which they know every corner, the small predators immediately hurry to the precise spot where a book has been moved or added to the others in their absence. Did the spot contain a small swirl of unaccustomed scent that might have attracted the weasel?"

From the same letter, let me also quote the following passage, in response to questions I posed in a previous article:

"Observations on polyandry, such as you have pointed out among finches, are unknown in the zoological literature. However, we do know that when all the males of a species do not find females with which to form steady couples, they will pursue in groups each one of the rare females in the vicinity. Hence the method, fairly widespread in certain parts of Germany, of exterminating sparrows—which consists of capturing the greatest possible number of sparrows in a given locale and then releasing only the males. They will then pursue and disturb the few females that remain to such a degree that they can no longer hatch their eggs and raise their brood. It has been supposed that this overpopulation of males is one of the reasons that led the females of some species of cuckoos and other birds to drop their eggs into strangers' nests and let them be hatched by others. Indeed, we know that for the European cuckoo, the males far outnumber the females, which isn't the case for certain North American cuckoos, which hatch their eggs themselves. 'Brood parasitism' (*Brutparasitismus*) would thus be a result of polyandry.[14]

"The method of exterminating sparrows that I have just mentioned may give rise to the question of whether certain phenomena of sterility observed in human societies of higher civilization might not have analogous causes to those that prevent the reproduction of sparrows, disturbed in this manner."

14. On this subject, see the very interesting pamphlet by Paul Sarasin, *Der Brutparasitismus des Kukucks und das Zahlenverhältnis der Geschlechter* (Brood parasitism in the cuckoo and the numerical proportion of the sexes) (1924).

The rest of my correspondent's letter, discussing the deviations of maternal instinct in animals, would take us too far afield. I will save it for a future article. Needless to say, I will gratefully accept any remarks sent to me about this subject.

☙ ☙ ☙

For J. Strohl, Dean of the
Faculty of Sciences in Zurich

I promised myself to return to this subject, which interests me greatly and has for a long time, for I was already discussing it at length before 1900. It was on the subject of the *Arabian Nights;* the examples of both Sinbad and the Calenders caused me to observe how their manly curiosity differs from that which is usually described in our Western literature. From Eve to Marienkind, Pandora to Bluebeard's wife, I scarcely see anything but female curiosity.[15] Perhaps I will be told that these notable examples also have Eastern origins. Certainly, but these are the ones that our literature and culture have adopted, examples not of boldness but of weakness.

I see alongside this curiosity weakness another curiosity that seems to me possibly the most hellish of the *energies* that Blake mentioned, which may lead a man to his ruin but leads humanity to progress. That's the one that interests me.

I suspected that in the animal, one might already recognize an embryonic form of curiosity at a stage where the two aspects are blended. This was the origin of the questions I put to my readers some months ago. The majority of answers tended to link curiosity, such as is displayed by certain animal species, either with the instinct for self-protection or with appetite, by which I mean the quest for food. The examples I was offered hardly seemed conclusive, and this explanation did not satisfy me at all. The most interesting of the examples, the ones most able to clarify the question a bit, were sent in by yourself, dear Monsieur Strohl; because of that I permit myself to inscribe your name

15. Tr. note: The literary examples Gide cites include *The Arabian Nights,* which contains such tales as "The Story of the Three Calenders, Sons of Kings, and of Five Ladies of Baghdad" and "The Seven Voyages of Sinbad the Sailor." Marienkind is the subject of a fairy tale collected by the Brothers Grimm.

at the top of these lines, and also because as a man of science, you have decided to look seriously on a man of letters' interest in research that at first glance seems beyond his competence. I even heard you deplore the fact that today the field of science is surrounded by such a barbed wire of technical terms that approaching it becomes nearly impossible for those who are not in the game. You feel that sometimes an amateur can shed new light on some points, and you recall that in the eighteenth century, literature and science were not so divided. Although in our day science has made noticeable progress precisely by specializing, I'd like it understood that what is important for me here is the study of the human spirit, for which not specializing too much is particularly vital; for it is often by the most winding roads that we manage to know it best. I am not trying to rediscover our emotions and the motives of our activity in animals. Rather, I'm looking for what sometimes already appears in rudimentary form in animals and in a more refined form in man: curiosity, for instance.

It seems to me that the primal form of curiosity (but does it then deserve that name?) is an animal's attraction to a static or moving point of light. No, we cannot call *curiosity* the attraction that unusual and shiny objects hold over certain beetles and lighthouses hold over winged creatures, insects and birds. Perhaps something analogous to this remains as part of curiosity, like the fascination, doubtless of the same kind, that makes a hummingbird rush into a snake's open maw. I believe that in its primal form, curiosity is fascination. I immediately noticed that this fascination leads the animal to its doom. It opposes all the other forces that may be linked to the "self-preservation instinct." I use these dated terms with a smile, but my meaning will be understood. I would say that it's the first appearance of a troublesome power that finds its most varied development in man—as long as these words don't imply an achieved goal, a finality that I refuse to see in nature, or at least not as simply as some eschatologists say. Let's say it more simply, that I see in man many mysteries that seem to originate in that fascination. No doubt it is fitting that we see curiosity as the most dangerous of all the motives that activate us, but it's also what pushes us to advancement, leads us to discovery, and brings us to the unknown. Without curiosity, humanity would have remained fixed in the Stone Age.

6. The Child Who Accuses Himself

For Jean Schlumberger

1. *An eight-year-old thief.*

"A painful and uniquely disturbing case has just been given to the jury at Aveyron. Here are the facts. Last November pieces of gold and banknotes—around five hundred francs—were stolen over several occasions from a hotel keeper in Salles-Curan.[16] He suspected a little shepherd boy, young Émile M——, *eight years old.* Bombarded with questions, the child finally confessed to the crime and stated that he had hidden the stolen money in a neighboring meadow. They went to the snow-covered meadow, yet after searching for several hours, they found nothing. When they returned to the village at nightfall, an observer, taking some twine from his pocket and throwing it at the child's head, shouted, 'Since he doesn't want to talk, we're going to hang him!' Terrified, the child then admitted he had given the entire sum to his father.

"The father was a postman. He was respected by all those who knew him, his supervisors, the police force, and local authorities, who all vouched for his honesty. He continued to proclaim his innocence; indeed, his son never dared repeat the accusation in front of him. However, he was suspended or dismissed from his responsibilities, since, not knowing what to think of the son's confession and perhaps believing in his guilt, he had signed promissory notes to the plaintiff, to pay him off bit by bit from his modest salary.

"The unfortunate postman and his son were brought together before the assize court under indictment for aggravated theft and aiding and abetting. At the hearing the child changed his story again by answering the president, who reminded him of his previous statements, that he didn't know what he was saying when he incriminated himself and that by informing against his father he was acting at the instigation of the hotel keeper's wife.

16. Tr. note: Salles-Curan is a scenic town in the Aveyron district, close to Roquefort and Rodez and about 650 kilometers from Paris.

"The director of public prosecutions dropped the accusation against the father and asked the jury to acquit him. But dealing harshly with the child, he asked for a conviction. The jury acquitted both defendants."

(*Le Temps,* June 29, 1910)

2. *A seventeen-year-old arsonist.*

"Some months ago we mentioned the crimes attributed to a seventeen-year-old boy, Marcel Gueyta, whom Father Andreau, an honorable diocesan parish priest from Tarbes, had sheltered and carefully raised, preparing him for the foreign missions.

"Extremely depraved despite a sickly sweet and prudish appearance, young Gueyta was accused of having robbed several churches and setting fires to mask the thefts.

"Thus on the night of last October 23–24, the Tarbes cathedral caught fire. The arsonist began by breaking open the sacristy poor box and then emptied the cruets holding white wine for mass while eating a number of hosts. After this profanation he set the fire, which fortunately was quickly put out.

"The investigation remained unsuccessful. It was certain that the criminal had entered through the belfry. That was all the preliminary investigation managed to reveal, when, on the night of November 13–14, another fire broke out in the sacristy of the Cadenac church, in the Saint-Félix region. The sacristy was completely destroyed and the church seriously damaged.

"Several poor boxes had been broken open.

"The next day, November 15, a third fire was set in a stable adjoining a church, using a handkerchief drenched in kerosene that was thrown into the building from outside.

"This time the investigation turned up footsteps leading to the presbytery where the Saint-Félix parish priest, Father Andreau, was preparing young Gueyta for a missionary career.

"The boy was arrested, and the inquest quickly revealed his responsibility for a fourth fire, which in the night of December 26–27, 1893, had completely destroyed his parents' home.

"A strange detail is that after each disaster, the court *received anonymous letters identifying young Gueyta as the arsonist. Now, when these accusations were reexamined, it was proven that Gueyta himself wrote them.*

"In March the young arsonist was brought before a jury at Tarbes.

"After three days of proceedings, the defense attorney, Monsieur Dasque, revealed to the court a previously unknown detail: Marcel Gueyta had shown signs of mental disturbance ever since the day when a hypnotist put him under during a public performance given at Tarbes.

"Monsieur Dasque asked the court to order an additional medical examination, and concurring with these conclusions, the court postponed the case to another date.

"Under these conditions, the case was brought up a second time.

"Despite the defense's efforts and the consistent medical opinion, the jury admitted Gueyta's responsibility and sentenced him to five years' imprisonment.

(Journal des débats, June 20, 1895)

7. The Wreck of the Steamer *Hilda*[17]

The shipwreck.

"On Sunday night a large steamship of the South Western Company, the *Hilda,* was lost with all hands on board along the rocks of Tour-

17. Tr. note: The wreck of the steamship *Hilda,* bound from Southampton, off Saint-Malo shortly after midnight on Saturday November 19, 1905, was a sensational news item in Brittany, inspiring much press coverage and souvenir postcards. Caught in a violent snowstorm, the ship hit the rocks called Les Portes to the west of a lighthouse at Grand Jardin. Only six survivors were picked up the following morning by the steamer *Ada,* not seven, as claimed in the newspaper clippings that Gide quotes; their names are recorded as Olivier Caroff of Roscoff, Tanguy Laot of Cléder, Louis Rozec of Plouzévédé, Paul-Marie Penn, Jean-Louis Mouster de La Feuillée, and the British stoker James Greender. In the account quoted in the *Le Temps* and reprinted by Gide, the Englishman Greender's name was apparently misspelled as "Grunter." See a novelized account of the tragedy based on the available facts: Yves Dufeil, *La Pierre des portes* (Paris: Éditions Solair, 1996).

Among the 131 persons aboard were a number of onion merchants from the area of Roscoff, called "les Johnnies." A thriving port city, Roscoff was the starting point for itinerant onion sellers who in those days left France to market their wares in England, where they were known as "Johnny Onions." See <http://www.multimania.com/mrrosko/asso02303.htm>.

du-Jardin, at the entrance to the Saint-Malo roadstead, resulting in many casualties.

"On Sunday morning the steamship *Ada,* leaving for Jersey at 8:30, observed at the channel entrance the masts of a steamship to which a number of exhausted men were clinging.

"The *Ada* lowered a dinghy into the sea, and with the help of a passing pilot boat seven men were saved. It was learned from them that the *Hilda* had encountered a storm during the night and ran aground on the rocks known as Les Portes, where she split apart and almost immediately sank like a stone.

"The *Hilda* had left Southampton on Friday evening. She should have reached Saint-Malo on Sunday evening. But at nightfall, the sky was covered in heavy black clouds, and snow threatened. Soon the storm broke, pushing snow flurries along with it, overtaking the ill-fated ship and making any maneuvers practically impossible.

"The night was opaque, and the unfortunate ship became lost in the darkness. Suddenly, a powerful shock was felt, followed by a kind of bang. The *Hilda* had just run aground on a rock—one of the rocks of Les Portes—and it is believed that, after the hull had splintered, an explosion went off in her smashed hold, and the ship sank with incredible speed.

"A large number of passengers had booked passage on the *Hilda.* Fifty-one onion merchants, returning to Brittany after their annual trip to England and Wales, and around ten cabin passengers and twenty-eight sailors, commanded by Captain Gregory, had gone aboard, a total of around one hundred people.

(*Le Temps,* November 21, 1905)

The account of the sailor Grunter.

"The correspondent of *The Daily Mail* at Saint-Malo interviewed the sailor Grunter, who told him the following:

"'I wasn't on duty, and I was sleeping in my bunk in the forecastle. There was a terrible snowstorm; the din of the elements seemed to drown out every other noise, when suddenly there was a powerful impact, followed by a grating sound.

"'Captain Gregory and the first mate were on the bridge, both of them perfectly calm.

"'Despite the darkness, I could see the tips of many needles of rock over the railings. It would have been useless to launch lifeboats into the sea, because they would have been dashed to bits.

"'The commander shouted at me through a megaphone to try to launch the other boats, but this was impossible, because the ship was rolling terribly and struck the rocks each time she moved. Then the commander yelled as loud as he could to everyone nearby him:

"'"For God's sake, my boys, try to launch a lifeboat for the women and children! Take the starboard boat."

"'But the rocks that rose on each side of the ship did not allow us to do that either, and just as we launched the starboard boat, the steamship began to sink.

"'There was no panic on board. I saw all of the women and children gathered together and two chambermaids putting life-belts on them; the women said nothing.

"'A little girl near me was sobbing. The French onion vendors helped to tie life-belts on the women; I saw all this while the ship was sinking and was struck by everyone's apparent calm.

"'We were in a snowstorm when the ship went down; I was thrown into the rigging, and I scaled the mainmast with the first mate and the cook.

"'The masts and spars were completely flattened; a certain number of French people who sought refuge on the other side were violently thrown into the water, before the mast went halfway up again. There were around twenty people in the tackle when the ship sank.

"'Below me, the first mate was asking me to climb higher, if possible. I went up to the shrouds, dying of the cold.

"'Around two hours after the ship sank, the ships' cook let go and slid into the water; the first mate held on until six o'clock, but then he fell forward onto the rigging, where his dead body remained hanging.

"'Another man died and remained hanging by one foot.

"'Shortly before dawn a Frenchman died in turn and fell, held up by one leg. I had to struggle the whole time against a violent desire to fall asleep.

"'Finally, at dawn, we saw the terrifying rocks on which we had been shipwrecked, and I noticed the *Ada* about a half-mile away.'"

(*Le Temps,* November 23)

8. A Superman Faces the Court

(Excerpted from *Vetchernyaya Moskva*
[*Moscow in the Evening*] of January 31, 1927)[18]

"Murders happen out of jealousy, greed, vengeance, or during a quarrel. Can you imagine that a murder would be committed simply to prove one's own willpower to oneself? That's the case of a young man, Slovookhotov, nineteen years old, who killed his girlfriend, Zina Gaukova, for no other reason.

"One day the students of a boarding school at Ufa[19] that Slovookhotov attended had a discussion, freely quoting Nietzsche and Dostoyevsky.

"As usual, Slovookhotov had an extreme opinion:

"'Man's will is infinite,' he stated. 'What I resolve to do, I do. I am capable of anything.'

"'But murder, you wouldn't do that.'

"'And why wouldn't I? I'm not like you, who wouldn't dare kill me, even if I absolved your responsibility in a document in which I would write that no one should be indicted for my death.'

"Zina Gaukova was present at this conversation. The young girl, sixteen years old, offered to write the said document, saying that she took Slovookhotov's statement seriously, whereas his comrades still saw it as nothing more than braggadocio.

"'And even after the murder,' Slovookhotov continued, 'I tell you that I would feel no remorse. I'd drink two bottles of beer, then go to the movies. That's all.'

18. Tr. note: *Vechernyaya Moskva* is one of Moscow's oldest daily newspapers, founded in 1923.

19. Tr. note: Ufa is the capital city of the Republic of Bashkortostan (Bashkiria), a center of religious life for Russian Muslims since the eighteenth century.

"An appointment was made. Slovookhotov bought a knife, sharpened it, and at the agreed-on time came to the boarding school. Zina was waiting for him.

"Slovookhotov was merry, joking and laughing.

"Zina Gaukova slipped away for a short time; as the other had insisted, she wrote the document and then sat in a chair while the other boarding-school students continued joking.

"Slovookhotov approached Zina. She repeated that she wasn't afraid. Then Slovookhotov pulled out his knife and stuck it deep into the young girl's chest.

"The stab was so fast and well-aimed that no one had time to stop the murderer's hand. Zina was wounded square in the heart. After having verified that she was dead, Slovookhotov went out, drank some beer in a restaurant, and then took in a movie.

"The next day he went to the police superintendent, to whom he showed the document written by Zina. He hoped that this paper would be enough to exonerate him or at least lessen the sentence to be served for his crime.

"A medical examination revealed Slovookhotov to be a perfectly normal man. The Bashkiria court sentenced Slovookhotov to nine years' imprisonment in strict isolation and limitation of his civil rights for five years.

(Sent by Monsieur Boris Griftsov)[20]

9. Parricide Because of Fear of Hell

One of the two had to die . . . and the son killed his father to escape committing suicide.

"Metz, October 26.—Telegr. *Matin.*—A parricide in particularly tragic circumstances has deeply stirred the town of Nilvange.[21]

---

20. Tr. note: Boris Aleksandrovich Griftsov [following the usual French and German transliteration, Gide spells his name "Griftzoff"] was a Russian man of letters who, together with Pavel Pavlovich Muratov, wrote *Nikolai Pavlovich Ulianov* (Moscow: State Publishing House, 1925). see also N. B. Tomashevskii's article in *The Modern Encyclopedia of East Slavic, Baltic, and Eurasian Literatures,* vol. 9, ed. Peter Rollberg (Gulf Breeze, Fla.: Academic International, 1989), s.v. "Griftsov, Boris Aleksandrovich."

21. Nilvange is a small town in the Moselle department, Lorraine region.

"Monsieur Émile Reiser, fifty years old, an accountant at the Wendel factory, was killed by his son Pierre, twenty-three years old.

"The murder was committed with disturbing brutality. The murderer approached his father, who was resting on a chaise longue, and stabbed him nine times in the head with a butcher knife.

"His head smashed in, Monsieur Reiser died three hours later.

"Interrogated by the examining magistrate, Monsieur Loubatière, the parricide stated that he regretted his act only because it dishonored his family.

"'Life was unbearable at our house,' he said, 'because of my father's constant complaints about my behavior. One of us had to die. I didn't want to kill myself, because I would have gone to hell. Now I can die in a state of grace.'

"When the judge pointed out that his father might not himself have been in that state at the moment of his death, the son replied indignantly:

"'I couldn't care less about that.'"

(*Le Matin,* October 29, 1925)

10. Cannibalism

All the newspapers discussed this case of cannibalism. We present the facts such as they were presented in *L'Éclair* of Montpellier (issue of March 10–11, 1927).

Eaters of human flesh.

"Suspected of murdering several people, a gang of Gypsies was arrested by the state police force of Moldava (Eastern Czechoslovakia).[22] The gang's leader, Alexander Filke, imprisoned along with twenty-five companions, was closely interrogated and finally made a confession so horrific that it surpassed anything imaginable.

"'We were the ones, all right,' he said, 'who killed the four or five missing people. We cut them into pieces and ate them at our campground.' With the human flesh, a little bland to the taste of one of the

22. Tr. note: Moldava is now part of the Slovak Republic.

accused, the cannibals made a goulash, the preparation of which was entrusted to the tribe's most expert female cooks. Paprika sauce, rice, and potatoes—nothing was spared to give the Hungarian national dish all its required highly seasoned flavor.

"One of the Gypsies, Rybar, a deaf-mute who could read and write, stated that the duly dismembered corpses that weren't immediately eaten were carefully salted to be stored. Four women and a small boy of thirteen thus served as food for the thieves.

" 'We didn't have anything to eat,' they offered as their only excuse, 'and that was all we had to keep from dying of hunger.' "

Cannibal Gypsies.

"The preliminary investigation of the case of Gypsy cannibalism, uncovered in eastern Czechoslovakia, is in full progress. The individuals arrested until now number twenty-six, including twelve men and fourteen women and children. They confessed to having perpetrated a dozen murders, the majority during the year 1926. Of the dozen victims, five men and four women were cut up and eaten.

"These wretched people showed a disconcerting cynicism. They obligingly explained how they managed to kill and dismember their victims and the ways in which they prepared the flesh. From the superstitious nature of their beliefs, quite close to primitive ideas of magic, one might have thought oneself dealing with a savage tribe in Africa. For example, one of the criminals explained that the brain was given by preference to the children, so that they would become more intelligent. Another one revealed that women's flesh was preferred by young people, who found it had a more dainty flavor and believed that it would add to their powers of seduction.

"Most of the arrested cannibals did not have haunts in Czechoslovakia. The victims largely seemed to be Hungarian."

11. A Blind Couple Divorces

The following news item, which we have translated from the *Frankfurter Zeitung,* has recently been reprinted in several Paris newspapers:

"A remarkable case of divorce proceedings occurred, a few days ago, in a Budapest courtroom. The plaintiff was a husband, twenty-eight years old, who went blind during the war and who lived thereafter by selling brushes. He had met his wife, sightless like him, in a home for the blind, and as he was told that she was young and pretty, he had married her. The couple lived together happily for one year, but then the honeymoon was over. Helpful friends, of the kind who always exist, told the husband that he had been duped in the marriage. His wife, and the facts would back this up, was not twenty years old at all but forty-eight and anything but pretty. This discovery infuriated the blind man. He bitterly reproached his wife and then ran to a judge to file a petition for divorce. He protested against the deception, and stated his resolve, despite his blindness, to have a young and charming wife.

"This divorce petition left the judge deeply perplexed, for a similar case had never happened before. The husband, as it would be shown, had absolutely no reason to reproach his wife apart from her age and lack of beauty. His request was not granted.

12. Incident at a Wedding

"A few days ago a wedding party arrived at the town hall of Rogerville (Seine-Inférieure) at the same time as Monsieur Desgenétais, the mayor, when a scandal occurred. A certain widow Confais, a tobacconist at Graville, arrived in a taxi. Confais threatened to kill her rival, the widow Couturier, née Léonie Frémont, forty-seven years old, if her ex-lover, the navigator Lévêque, fifty-five years old, married Couturier. The mayor ordered the village policeman to eject the jealous lover. Once calm had been restored, Monsieur Desgenétais read the code's articles to the bride and groom and then, addressing the groom, asked him:

"'Will you take Léonie Frémont to be your wedded wife?'

"To which, still upset from the scene that had just taken place, the groom asked the mayor:

"'What do you think I should do?'

"The wedding party broke into laughter, along with the groom himself. The mayor asked the question a second time; this time Monsieur Lévêque replied with a decisive no. The wedding was over. As the navigator was passing by, the widow Confais invited him to join her."

(Le Temps, August 5, 1922)

13. A Pharmacist's Confinement

"While mental tests of the pharmacist Brunet continue, his wife is questioned by the examining magistrate Bourdeaux. She states that she did not seek her husband's confinement but merely agreed to it because he caused some serious worries for her and her daughter, and thus she followed the advice she had been given to put her husband in a clinic. Here is a summary of the questioning that she underwent yesterday:

"'We only felt safe when he was in the clinic,' said Madame Brunet.

"'But he had returned totally cured, and the investigation showed that since then, no new events justified your second request for confinement.'

"'Oh, he was only partially cured, as Monsieur Guillevic noticed as soon as he returned to the house. One day at the table, whereas he usually kept quiet, he suddenly started to talk about museum guards. Yet we had not spoken of these humble civil servants on that day nor on previous days. We looked at each other at that moment, Guillevic and myself, and after lunch, the aide told me: "He is certainly quite mad, and it's time to lock him up!"'

"'Really, ma'am,' exclaimed the judge, 'and nothing else happened? Then it took very little to push you to grave measures to deprive your husband of his liberty!'

"Next the judge asked her why she had not consulted with Doctor Lévy, who had drafted the first certificate, instead of applying to Doctor Benon, whom she did not know. Madame Brunet replied that she relied entirely on Guillevic, who had advised confinement for Monsieur Brunet."

(Le Temps, June 10, 1910)

14. The Pleasure of Sports

For Jean Prévost[23]

The Jeffries-Johnson Match.[24]

"In fifteen rounds Johnson defeated Jeffries, the former world champion who, after six years of retirement, had chosen to return to the ring to take the boxing title away from the black race.

"The sensational match that took place in Reno, Nevada, fascinated the Americans, captivated the British, and greatly interested a certain number of Frenchmen. The results would be known in Paris around midnight, as we were told yesterday. As the crowds were leaving the theaters, the news of Johnson's victory spread very quickly, from a cable that our Parisian colleague *The Daily Mail* had just received. It was the subject of conversation at the majority of late suppers, even though details were still sketchy.

"Here, to describe the surroundings of the match and the environment of Reno, is the article by *The Daily Telegraph*'s correspondent:

"Jeffries got up at 8:00 A.M. and for breakfast had five lamb chops. Johnson awoke an hour later and ate half a chicken. In accordance with the rules, they were examined by doctors, who found them both in perfect health.

"The two champions then made more-or-less grandiloquent statements expressing their certainty of victory.

"The crowd began to head for the arena shortly before noon; the weather was splendid. The amphitheater was located about a twenty-minute walk outside Reno. On the road was the strangest mob imag-

23. Tr. note: Gide's friend Jean Prévost (1901–44) was an energetic young writer who died fighting in the French resistance at the Battle of Vercors. His first article in the *N.R.F.*, "Journée du pugiliste" (1924), was about boxing. He published *Plaisirs des sports. Essais sur le corps humain* (Paris: Gallimard, 1925), the title of which Gide borrows for the present chapter. He was nine years old at the time of the match Gide discusses here.

24. Tr. note: Called "The Fight of The Century," the July 4, 1910, bout in Reno, Nevada, between Jack Johnson, the first black heavyweight champion, and Jim Jeffries retains its aura. It is still the most internationally famous event that ever occurred in Reno, which hosted the fight after the city of San Francisco canceled the "brutal exhibition" on moral grounds.

inable: sportsmen, politicians, cowboys, bankers, miners in red jackets, Texan colonists, Japanese, and Chinamen. The noise was hellish: automobile horns, shouts from watermelon vendors, and bookmakers yelling out the odds.

"Johnson had received death threats in the event that he should win, so all suspicious characters—and there were many in this half-wild region—were searched at the entrance to the amphitheater, and all revolvers were confiscated. They were asked to leave them in the cloakroom in exchange for a number, as is done in Europe for umbrellas. Bottles of whiskey, knives, and American-style knuckle dusters also had to be handed in.

"It must be added that for extra security, the police sent a considerable number of detectives into all the bars and other shady places, with the order to arrest any suspicious characters immediately. The prisons of Reno were soon full.

"All the regular police were on foot patrol. A certain number of additional hardy fellows had been requisitioned as volunteer policemen and were stationed throughout the amphitheater, assigned to immediately eject any rowdies. We must add incidentally that a certain number of these auxiliary workers had to be arrested for picking pockets almost immediately after they started work. But that is a mere detail.

"The amphitheater was already filled several hours before the match. In honor of Independence Day, American flags waved from all sides. At every moment 'messenger boys'[25] came and shouted out the odds. Around noon they were at two-to-one in favor of Jeffries.

"At one o'clock the Reno Army Band took its place and played the national anthem.

"Jeffries arrived at 1:35, followed five minutes later by Johnson.

"Jeffries and Johnson, greeted by a whirlwind of applause and surrounded by bestial shouts, entered the arena. It was 2:30, Nevada time. At this moment an immense throng was in the amphitheater, at least 18,000 people, while 15,000 others outside stamped their feet, bawled, and swore to get a seat. To no avail.

"Billy Jordan, the announcer, had already appeared in front of the

25. Tr. note: The term appears in English in the original.

crowd at 1:45 to declare in a loud voice that Johnson was in his dressing room, preparing for the great battle. 'The fighters,' he added, 'will make at least 50,000 francs as bonus.'

"The sum taken in at the gate reached 1,250,000 francs.

"Soon afterward a parade of champions and ex-champions marched across the platform: Bob Fitzsimmons, John Sullivan, Jake Kilrain, Tommy Burns, Gotch the wrestler, and other sports celebrities, while a storm of shouts and applause raged through the arena.[26] Several of these champions wanted to say a few words, which slightly delayed the arrival of Jeffries and Johnson.

"The fight began at 2:45.

"Here is an analysis of the key rounds:

"*Fifth round:* After a clinch (body to body) Jeffries connects with a right. Johnson retaliates with two lefts to the mouth. Jeffries bleeds profusely. Johnson adds two more lefts to the mouth.

"*Sixth round:* Johnson scores two straight lefts to the face. Then immediately, after a clinch, he lands a swing at Jeffries's face, opening a previous cut, and another punch to the ear that backs Jeffries against the ropes. At this moment Jeffries attempts a swing to the body, but Johnson returns a terrifying right cross, after which comes another clinch. Jeffries's eye starts to swell shut. Jeffries is bleeding profusely from his mouth and eye.

"*Seventh round:* Jeffries follows Johnson all around the ring. Johnson lands another straight right to the mouth and a jab to the eye.

"Johnson is going at full force. Jeffries, by contrast, looks exhausted. Johnson lands another powerful straight right.

"*Eighth round:* Jeffries's desperate attack is stopped by a left to the ear and an uppercut, immediately followed by a left to the ribs that makes him swing around.

"*In the tenth round* Jeffries's eye is almost entirely closed. Jeffries manages to land a left cross to the chin of Johnson, who starts to bleed.

26. Tr. note: Bob Fitzsimmons (1863–1917) was boxing's first triple world champion; John L. Sullivan (1858–1918), "The Boston Strong Boy," was the first great American sports idol; Jake Kilrain (John Joseph Killion; 1859–1937), was declared heavyweight champion of the world by the *Police Gazette* in 1887; Tommy Burns (1881–1955) was a Canadian fighter; and Frank Gotch (c. 1876–1917) was an Iowa-born world-champion heavyweight wrestler.

"*In the eleventh round* Jeffries's face is covered in blood. He continues to defend himself bravely.

"*In the twelfth round* Johnson lands a left to the ear. A clinch in which Johnson is rather severely manhandled but that doesn't prevent him from landing two blows to the face, one right and one left. Then he lands a straight to Jeffries's nose, and soon after, two more rights to the nose, and finally a left hook square in the face.

"*In the thirteenth round,* after a clinch, Johnson lands one to the nose. Another clinch; Johnson lands two hard lefts to the face of Jeffries, who is pushed back and whose head is knocked back by an uppercut. Jeffries lands a left; Johnson makes Jeffries stagger under the weight of three powerful straights right after two jabs to the face. Jeffries's face is now in a piteous condition. Every second, Jeffries takes another blow.

"*In the fourteenth round* Johnson hits his nose, and blood flows again. Then he lands two blows in a clinch. Jeffries focuses on his lower guard, but that doesn't prevent him from getting two blows to the face. All the blows from Johnson are astonishingly precise.

"Jeffries lands a left to the face in a clinch. Johnson lands a few more very hard blows. Jeffries shakes his head continuously to dodge the numerous blows launched by the Negro. He holds up in the clinch, where he makes good use of his left.

"*In the fifteenth round,* after a clinch that follows an attempt by Jeffries to hit Johnson in the face, Johnson quickens the pace of the fight, knocking Jeffries down with two blows to the jaw, a left and a right.

"Jeffries gets up again before a count of ten but immediately falls back down again and is still on his knees when the referee counts ten.

"A knockout is declared despite the shouting mob, despairing to see the white man defeated.

"Monsieur Hamilton Fyfe, special correspondent for *The Daily Mail,* telegraphs that Johnson proved his undeniable superiority through the entire fight. To speak in the language of boxing aficionados, Jeffries 'wasn't there.' Johnson finished him off with a final uppercut. But his hooks and left uppercuts during clinches really floored the former world champion. By the sixth round, the experts' minds were made up.

"Jeffries's defeat was acutely felt. But instead of changing bitterness into wild hatred of Johnson, the Americans attacked Jeffries. Now that he was beaten, the crowd bitterly reproached him for his defeat.

"'If you're not ready to fight,' it was heard from all corners, 'don't get into the ring.'

"'By his mad presumption,' it is still said in Reno, 'Jeffries humiliated the entire white race.'

"Johnson won 303,000 francs, plus the income earned on the film reproduction rights. The whole sum was over one million. Jeffries earned 202,000 francs.

"Johnson, the victor, son of a Negro Protestant minister, is thirty-two years old. His adversary, the former world champion Jeffries, is thirty-five years old. He is also the son of a Protestant minister.

(Le Temps, July 6, 1910)

❦ ❦ ❦ The Confined Woman of Poitiers

> "I've discovered that all man's miseries derive from a single thing, which is not being able to sit quietly in a room."
> —Pascal, *Pensées,* 94 (Massis ed.)

> "Quite often it suffices to add up a number of little facts, very simple and natural when taken individually, to arrive at a monstrous result."
> —*The Counterfeiters,* 1.4.51.

Preface

I have some scruples about putting my name to the narrative of this strange story. In the wholly impersonal account I am going to present, my only concern was to organize the documents that I was able to collect and stand back, out of their way.

This is how, in 1901, *La Vie illustrée* introduced its readers to the strange case that will concern us:

Hidden Tragedies
The Confined Woman of Poitiers

In a quiet and peaceful street in Poitiers, with the monastic name of rue de la Visitation, lived an upper-middle-class family who were universally honored in the region. The widow Monnier, née Demarconnay, from a highly aristocratic Poitiers family, lived there with her son, Monsieur Marcel Monnier, a former subprefect of Puget-Théniers, at Seize-Mai.[1]

Tr. note: For more on the case, see Jean-Marie Augustin, *L'Histoire véridique de la Séquestrée de Poitiers* (Paris: Fayard, 2001), and for its legal aspects, see Jean Pradel and André Varinard, *Les Grands Arrêts du droit criminel,* 3d ed. (Paris: Sirey, 1992), vol. 1, 309–16.

1. The confined woman of Poitiers was named Blanche Monnier. Gide changed her name to Mélanie Bastian to protect innocent members of the family. In 1930 Blanche Monnier's niece, Marie-Dolorès Monnier, was still alive. In subsequent Gallimard editions, the name Blanche Monnier and those of her relatives were sporadically altered, creating a confusing effect. In the present first-ever translation into English, the real names of the individuals have been used throughout in a uniform way.

Madame Monnier Demarconnay, seventy-five years old, lived in the house she had shared with her husband, who had been the head of the arts faculty in the old provincial city. Her son married a Spanish lady with a temperament livelier than his own and returned alone to Poitiers. He lived in a building facing his mother's. There was a third family member, a daughter named Blanche, who was joyous and playful until age twenty-five, when she suddenly disappeared. Mental illness was mentioned. Madame Monnier first had her placed in a clinic and then took her in out of devotion and Christian charity, caring for her selflessly, with the help of an old maidservant, behind closed shutters in the sad house where visitors were no longer received. Madame Renard, the old maidservant, forty years in her employers' service, received a medal from the Committee of Good Works at the request of Monsieur Marcel Monnier, who, conscious of his partial blue blood, went by the name of Monnier de Marconnay. It was a prize for virtue that honored both the old servant and her highly virtuous masters. But the virtuous Madame Renard died, and new servants entered the house, that strange house with a certain window whose shutters were padlocked from the outside and from which muffled, distant screams could sometimes be heard. When night fell in that stern household, one of the maids was pleased to welcome a sturdy soldier, a lieutenant from the garrison. This warrior, more adept with a feather duster and polishing brush than a bayonet or rifle, lacked Madame Renard's discretion and knew that anonymous letters rarely compromise their authors. So he wrote one. Thus, the public prosecutor's office, served in Poitiers by an uncurious police department, learned: (1) that Mademoiselle Blanche Monnier was by no means mad and (2) that she had been kept in a state of seclusion for twenty-four years in a filthy room—the stern room with padlocked shutters—from which she never emerged and where she lived amid filth, vermin, worms, and rats, in total darkness and almost starving. Belatedly, these gentlemen of the magistracy, who greatly respected the right-minded Monnier family—just as everyone respected them—must have been deeply troubled. They stepped in, forced open the door, and found the unfortunate creature lying in an indescribable hovel.

The reasons? This is what is said in Poitiers: Mademoiselle Blanche Monnier, around her twenty-fifth year, fell in love and gave herself. It is believed that a child was born, the fruit of her love. It is also thought that the child was done away with. Both to punish the poor girl for what the world calls an error and above all to keep her from talking, the pure, honorable, and excellent Madame Monnier Demarconnay, aided in this by the silence of her worthy son, locked Blanche away forever in the dirty room where she refused to die and where she had now been discovered, twenty-four years later.

It was a horrible drama of prejudices, respectability, and excessive virtue—a virtue based on hideous conventions—but even more abominable is the cowardice of the witnesses who come forward in large numbers today but who were fiercely silent for a quarter-century, when it might have seemed more perilous to speak up.

Discretion is truly still a virtue, and for twenty-four years that virtue, also excessive and cowardly, was the criminal accomplice of the cruel virtue of the widow Monnier Demarconnay and her son, the right-minded subprefect.

Even from this article's tone, an echo of the public outrage at the time can be perceived. How could this monstrous-seeming case, in which Madame Monnier and her son appeared clearly guilty from the start, have ended with the accused being acquitted? Doubtless this will become understandable by reading the following.

Chapter 1

On May 22, 1901, the attorney general of Poitiers received an anonymous letter, dated May 19, that read:

Monsieur Attorney General:
I have the honor to inform you of an exceptionally serious occurrence. I speak of a spinster who is locked up in Madame Monnier's house, half-starved, and living on a putrid litter for the past twenty-five years—in a word, in her own filth.

On May 23 at 2:30, on receipt of the anonymous letter, the chief superintendent of police at Poitiers, on the orders of and investigating for the district attorney, appeared at 21 rue de la Visitation.

One of the two maidservants in Madame Monnier's employ, Mademoiselle Dupuis, answered the doorbell:

"Madame Monnier?"

"Madame is not receiving. She is confined to bed."

"Please tell the widow Monnier that I am the chief superintendent and that I absolutely must speak with her."

So the servant went up to the second floor and returned a few moments later, saying:

"Sir, madame asks you to speak with her son, who lives across the street."

So the chief superintendent went to knock on Monsieur Marcel Monnier's door. At first, however, he was told there that Monsieur Monnier was also unwell.

"It's quite odd," replied the chief superintendent, "how everyone in both these houses is unwell. Tell your master that I am the chief superintendent, and I have an important message for him."

The chief superintendent was received by Monsieur Marcel Monnier. He told him:

"An anonymous letter has denounced your mother for having confined your sister, Blanche Monnier, to her bed for twenty-five years, amid putrid rot; the letter adds that her room's window is padlocked. Indeed, when I just arrived at the domicile, I noticed a shuttered window on the third floor. Would you take me to your sister?"

"And who might you be?" asked Monsieur Monnier.

"I am the chief superintendent, as your maid must have told you."

"What you have just said," continued Monsieur Monnier, "is a terrible calumny. I am not involved in this matter in any way; what's more, my mother and sister live together in a house apart from my own. Respecting the wishes of my mother, who insists on being mistress in her own house, I never involve myself in her business."

"Be that as it may," the chief superintendent interrupted, "I am anxious to learn about it *de visu*. The best way to vindicate yourself, sir, is to let me see your sister and speak with her."

"I cannot let you see her without first calling her doctor. He will be able to say if you can go into her room without disturbing her. For the last ten years or so, my sister has been afflicted with a pernicious fever and must not receive any visitors."

Answering the chief superintendent's questions, Monsieur Marcel Monnier gave his age, fifty-three years old, and his profession: doctor of law and former subprefect. His sister's age: fifty-two years old. Madame Monnier had no other children. Moreover, Marcel Monnier stated, his sister was in no way abandoned; he himself went to see her several times a day. He protested the denunciation of his mother and said that he would report the matter to the district attorney.

The Chief Superintendent then pointed out that the best way of disproving the calumny was to show him into Mademoiselle Monnier's room without further delay. He had been able to see from outside that the shutters on a third-floor room were kept closed with a chain, which lent some credence to the anonymous letter's denunciations.

Marcel Monnier seemed ready to agree, but first he had to obtain authorization from his mother, who decided everything in her own house.

Therefore he went to her, accompanied by the chief superintendent. Madame Monnier hesitated for a long time and then, after the chief superintendent insisted, finally agreed.

"Monsieur Marcel Monnier," said the chief superintendent, "led us to the third floor, to a room lit by a single window facing a courtyard. The light was dim and the air so foul that we were immediately forced to leave the room, but not before noting that the window's shutters were closed and secured by a padlocked chain and that the window was hermetically sealed, with weather stripping over every joint.

"We went into the room again, trying to open the window to let in some air, but were prevented from doing so by Monsieur Monnier, who told us that this would bother his sister.

"We also noted that his unfortunate sister, whom we could not see, was lying on a poor pallet and covered with a blanket—all repugnantly filthy; across this pallet ran insects and vermin feeding on the feces on the unfortunate woman's bed. We tried to uncover her face, but she clung to the blanket, which covered her entirely, shrieking loudly, like a wild woman.

"Unable to stay in the room any longer, due to its repulsive filthiness, we withdrew and questioned the two maids."

At five o'clock on the same day, it was the turn of the examining magistrate, Judge Du Fresnel, to visit the room. After his first notes, which concurred with those of the chief superintendent, he added:

"We immediately gave the order to open the casement window. This was done with great difficulty, for the old dark-colored curtains fell down in a heavy shower of dust. To open the shutters, it was necessary to remove them from their right hinges.

"As soon as light entered the room, we noticed, in the back, lying on a bed, her head and body covered by a repulsively filthy blanket, a woman whom Monsieur Marcel Monnier identified as his sister, Mademoiselle Blanche Monnier. The unfortunate woman was lying completely naked on a rotten straw mattress. All around her was formed a sort of crust made from excrement, fragments of meat, vegetables, fish, and rotten bread. We also saw oyster shells and bugs running across Mademoiselle Monnier's bed. The latter was covered with vermin. We spoke to her; she shouted and clutched her bed, trying to better cover her face. Mademoiselle Monnier was frighteningly emaciated; her hair formed a thick matting that had not been combed or untangled for a long time.

"The air was so unbreathable, the odor given off by the room was so rank, that it was impossible for us to stay any longer to proceed with other note-taking."

Judge Du Fresnel decided to send Mademoiselle Blanche Monnier to the hospital immediately. Because she owned no underwear or clothes, he had her wrapped up in a blanket and then ordered that her room be disinfected as much as was possible. At six o'clock the door was officially sealed.

"Before leaving the house," continued the examining magistrate, "we proceeded to visit the inhabited rooms. The dining room was properly furnished, the kitchen was well maintained, and the staircase clean. The widow Monnier's room was disorderly, but we noted that it was not at all dirty; the furniture was in good condition, the bed comfortable, and the bed, sheets, and covers all very clean. The elder Madame Monnier, who is seventy-five years old, was garbed in a dressing gown decorated with little black and white squares; she wore a fluted white cap. Everything was well tended; she was carefully groomed; in short, she did not seem to be a woman who neglected her personal cleanliness."

At three o'clock the next day, the examining magistrate returned to the more-or-less disinfected room, where the odor was still very strong, and proceeded to complete the notes that he had been forced to abandon on the first day because of the room's stench:

The room measured 5 meters, 40 centimeters by 3 meters, 40 centimeters; the window was 1 meter, 60 centimeters by 0 meters, 98 centimeters. The furniture included,

1. to the right, near the door, a commode without drawers;

2. two sets of shelves made of deal, situated to the right and left of a mantelpiece made of black marble; on the right one were four empty bottles, three cans of food, a lotto set, and two screws; the left one, closed off by strips of ticking, held no objects, but its corners were covered with thick spiderwebs; on the mantelpiece stood a small statue of the Virgin Mary;

3. an iron bed in front of the commode: the sheets and covers were clean, this being where one of the two servants slept;

4. in front of the left-hand shelf, a small bedstead covered with a straw mattress and old soiled rags;

5. a couch frame on which were piled rags and tatters crawling with vermin;

6. six straw-bottomed chairs, of which four were in fairly good condition;

7. finally, Mademoiselle Monnier's wooden bed, containing a rotten straw mattress, a sheet folded into quarters to hold excrement, an old pillow, and placed between the sheet and mattress, an appallingly filthy blanket. The bed is covered with a sort of paste formed of excrement, scraps of meat, vegetables, and rotting bread. At the foot of the bed, an extremely dirty square of linoleum. The floor is eaten away. A hole of 32 centimeters long by 5 centimeters wide near the wall and another hole at the level of the bed allow the movement of rats. Between the bed and the left-hand shelf, a little case filled with old books, covered, like everything else, with a thick coat of dust. The wallpaper is practically gone. The walls were once papered in grayish blue with brown and dark blue squares; they are now almost bare. Many inscriptions remain, rather hard to decipher. We finally manage to read one of them:

> *"Make beauty, nothing of love or freedom, always solitude. One must live and die in jail all one's life."*

On May 25, at nine o'clock in the morning, the police superintendent proceeded to the confiscation of the following items:

"One quilt, partially rotted; a rotted pillow adhering to it, as well as
diverse other bits of rags joined to each other by feces, scraps of food
of all kinds, mixed with a great quantity of insects (the whole thing was
wrapped up for us in a white sheet lent by the family); one white blanket with red stripes; a yellow blanket that covered the confined woman;
one pillow; one blanket with blue stripes; one newly washed rag; one
coverlet in white with blue flowers; one more old blanket with red
stripes; one ticking doubled and placed against the window as curtains;
one piece of blanket with green stripes; one old rag that had been used
for placing underneath Mademoiselle Monnier; a piece of white linen
soiled with fecal matter; a bedsheet folded into eighths, on which rested
part of the victim's body; one newspaper containing food residue—
newspaper provided by us; various other food debris that we wrapped
in a paper and that, like the previously mentioned material, fell off the
bed at the moment of the seizure operation; these aforementioned
objects were placed in a box.

"One straw mattress, partially rotted, which we wrapped in a packing sheet; one cot that we divided into five packets; two shutters connected by a chain held together by a padlock; one trunk into which we
placed thirty-seven volumes found on the shelves of her room; one
student's basket containing notebooks and a great quantity of notes
written in pencil(?); in the same trunk we also placed a padlock closed
with a length of chain, two statuettes of the Virgin Mary, one doll's
head, one rosary, one ten-centime coin, and five pencil stubs found on
and under her pallet.

"One door to the victim's room, recently repaired; the frame of the
aforementioned door; one jar containing insects, representing around
5 to 10 percent of those found on the bed of Blanche Monnier;[2] one

2. The newspapers vied with one another to emphasize the diversity, enormity, and hid-
eousness of the worms that crawled on Blanche Monnier's bed. One might have thought that
they were a surprising, unknown form of animal life. In fact, Monsieur Léger, professor at
the Poitiers School of Medicine and director of the bacteriological laboratory , immediately
saw that the worms collected in the formalin jar belonged to only two species: (1) the long-
est, with the appearance of yellow worms, were *Tenebrio larvae* (insect beetle), a larva more
commonly known as the "mealworm"; and (2) larder beetle larva, or *Dermestes lardarius,*
another insect beetle that habitually lives in pantries, where it feeds on food debris of all kinds.

white blanket; one piece of wallpaper from the corridor containing the words: 'some the children there are some of them who are much preferred,' etc., etc., and finally one hair braid belonging to Blanche Monnier, weighing 2 kilos, 70; this hair was cut off when she arrived at the hospital."

As long as this list may seem, we have no fear of reproducing it in its entirety, regretting only that it was not even more complete; for example, we would like to have known the titles of the thirty-seven confiscated volumes and the nature of the "notes written in pencil" mentioned in the report. Recently we have appreciated the specific eloquence of objects in General Diterik's account of the seizure carried out on the little room of the Ipatieff house in Ekaterimbourg.[3]

All these objects are witnesses, and their testimony teaches us as much, and more simply, than that of the living witnesses whom we would soon hear.

But first we will hear the accused.

Chapter 2

Madame Monnier and her son were arrested on the afternoon of May 24. We will present all the information that we have been able to ob-

3. Count Kokovtzoff: "The Truth about the Ekaterimbourg Tragedy," *Revue des deux mondes*, October 1, 1929.

[Tr. note: General Dietrichs (Gide uses the Russian form—Diteriks—of the name) served as commander-in-chief for Admiral Aleksandr Vailiyevich Kolchak (1874–1920), who supported Alexander Kerensky's provisional government after the Russian Revolution.

The Ipatiev House: In 1918 the Bolsheviks placed the Romanov royal family, including the tsar, his wife, and children, under house arrest at the former home of a local businessman, Nikolai Ipatiev, in Ekaterinburg. There they were murdered, in circumstances that became clear only in 1989, although many sympathetic supporters, such as General Dietrichs, offered detailed descriptions of the Ipatiev House and what was found there after the Romanovs mysteriously vanished on July 17. On July 25 the White Army entered Ekaterinburg, and officers found rubbish and odds and ends of the family's possessions strewn around the house. Gide mentions this debris in reference to the objects discovered in Blanche Monnier's room. Accounts of the Ipatiev house included the information that there was writing on the wall on the cellar, undecipherable inscriptions as well as a line from Heinrich Heine's poem "Baltazar," about the biblical King Belshazzar. Blanche Monnier's writing on the wallpaper was a comparable detail. See Robert K. Massie, *The Romanovs* (New York: Random House, 1995.)

Count Vladimir Nikolaevich Kokovtsov (b. 1853), a Russian minister of finance, wrote memoirs of his life in the Russian civil service, including his post-Revolutionary arrest, imprisonment, and exile.]

tain about these two disconcerting figures later on. First let's hear Marcel Monnier at the president's interrogation (session of October 8, 1901; see *Journal de l'ouest,* October 10).

Q: "Starting in 1875, Doctor Guérineau observed that your sister, Blanche, was unable to take care of herself. Her room was filthy, and your sister was dressed in dirty clothes. She was tended by a woman named Fazy, who died in 1896."

A: "That's correct."

Q: "When your sister's condition worsened, your mother had the doors locked. After the death of the woman Fazy, there came a long line of maids who would not agree to stay in such an environment. Your sister no longer left her room; she demanded her freedom; she made appeals, up to the moment when the police found her, in May 1901."

A: "All that is true."

Q: "The chief superintendent came; you presented obstacles to his getting into your sister's room."

A: "No, but I wanted to get my mother's permission; no objection on my part."

Q: "Yet you said that your sister was suffering from pernicious fever. You mentioned your social standing and former titles."

A: "It was never my thought to prevent the chief superintendent from entering."

. . . .

The president orders the record of the police report read aloud.

Q: "Aren't you impressed?"

A: "I am horrified; but I never saw anything except from outside. Knowing that Blanche was nude, I never looked at her, out of a sense of decency. I only saw her hair."

Q: "So this situation is completely new to you?"

A: "I didn't imagine it. I was far from thinking it."

Q: "Your sister, taken to the hospital, showed pleasure at being washed and breathing clean air. She exclaimed, 'How lovely it is.'"[4]

A: "All the time that she stayed in her mother's house, Blanche had

4. What the president does not say is that when they came to take her to the hospital, Blanche Monnier also shouted, "Anything you like, but don't take me away from my dear little grotto."

a great aversion to light. She couldn't stand it; it was according to her instincts."

Q: "You only had to show a sign of will."

A: "My mother was mistress of her household."

Q: "At the hospital, it was observed that your sister was very modest, very well-behaved. Why then, in that case, these measures of protection?"

A: "These measures date back very far. It was my late father who started them."

Q: "I saw in the file that nothing was done against her will" (Blanche's or Madame Monnier's? the sentence is ambiguous).

A: "Yes, to avoid terrible scenes."

Q: "You must not have forgotten that you were dealing with a madwoman; all the more reason to impose care on her, which moreover she accepted with pleasure at the hospital."

A: "I trusted the servants."

Q: "Your sister was well fed, if one can say that of a person who is offered something, without being checked to see if she has eaten it."

A: "That was the maids' duty."

Q: "Did you sometimes go to see your sister?"

A: "Yes; sometimes I tried to distract her,[5] but conversation was difficult.

Q: "In her moments of lucidity, what did she say?"

A: "I can only say this: often I asked my mother to put my sister in a nursing home. Near the window, I would read the *Journal de la Vienne.* I was never disturbed by the odor."

(We will return later to this last claim. Several questions and answers follow in which Marcel Monnier repeats that he never realized the frightful state of neglect in which his sister was left.)

Q: "You say that you suggested to your mother that she put your sister in a nursing home. Why didn't you take action?"

A: "I insisted so much that my mother threw me out."

Q: "How did you get along with your mother?"

A: "I had great filial respect for her. But there was always conflict

5. Another interrogation will inform us that Marcel Monnier spent a fairly long time every day beside his sister.

between us—sometimes about money matters, sometimes about my sister."

Q: "You gave in to your mother, but weren't there some ticklish questions?"

A: "I am too high-minded to stoop to such baseness."

Answering a question from the president, Marcel Monnier says that he has neither a good sense of smell nor good vision. He doesn't even recognize his friends in the street.

Q: "Yet you write. You paint from nature."

A: "In my watercolors there is a big difference between my picture and the original."

Q: "You are blamed for never having tried to resolve your sister's situation. You decided to let her stay moaning on a filthy dung heap."

A: "I've never had anything but feelings of affection and devotion for my sister."

With this phrase, the interrogation ended.

The examining magistrate registered as evidence at the court clerk's office not only the material seized from Blanche Monnier's room but also the following, taken from Monsieur Monnier study:

1. one hardback notebook bearing the following inscriptions: "Aid for wounded soldiers—Central Committee of Paris—list of wounded former soldiers having requested aid from the Red Cross organization, living in Poitiers or the department of la Vienne";

2. one bundle of documents enclosed in green folder bearing the inscription: Saint Vincent de Paul Society;

3. fifty-six watercolors made by Monsieur Monnier, enclosed in a green folder.

4. fifty-four drawings in pencil or watercolor made by Monsieur Monnier and enclosed in a green folder;

5. one draft of an obituary article about the Count de T——;

6. notes of a speech given by Monsieur Marcel Monnier on May 16, 1896, on aid to soldiers wounded before the Geneva convention and during the war of 1870;

7. one sheet of school paper found on Monsieur Monnier's desk, on which one reads:

"We are anxious to provide our readers with exact information that will shed true light on the case that has thrown our city into acute emotion by questioning the responsibility of one of our most sympathetic fellow citizens." This beginning of an article was in the same handwriting as all the other confiscated documents.

Questioned another time, Marcel Monnier said further:

"The inscriptions that have been pointed out, written on the wall of the room that my sister occupied before 1882(?) . . . , these inscriptions, which are mostly about the Sacred Heart of Jesus and Mary, are insignificant. Although I do admit that they indicate some religious thoughts in my sister's mind, which I ascribe to hallucinations. I must say that my sister never expressed any desire to take her vows."

About other inscriptions, written by Blanche Monnier on the walls of the other room that she inhabited, after 1882 (year of the death of Monsieur Monnier, her father), inscriptions dealing with *stolen freedom* and *solitude,* and one sentence in particular, "*One must live and die in prison all one's life,*" Marcel Monnier responds:

"There are psychological phenomena that I will not try to explain; moreover, I accorded so little importance to the inscriptions on the walls that I didn't even read them."

Q: "It emerges from the testimony of several witnesses that your sister often was heard screaming and pleading, including clear mention of words such as *police, court, freedom,* and also *prison.* On August 16, 1892, Monsieur Jacob heard the following words: 'What have I done to be locked up; I don't deserve this horrible torture. God must not exist then, to let his creatures suffer in this way? And no one to come to my rescue!'"

A: "All these screams had no meaning; in my sister's mouth, these words have no value; she only said them at moments of crisis and madness. She never called for help or demanded her freedom in front of me. I simply noted that she used very foul expressions during her fits of anger, notably the word *sh——*; she seemed to be talking to an imaginary being; it was impossible to make her see reason; the more one talked to her, the more she flew into a rage."

Q: "How do you explain that this overexcitement and rage suddenly stopped as soon as your sister was admitted to hospital, to be replaced by a calm that has not wavered for a moment?"

A: "It's probable that the great emotion she experienced delivered a salutary shock to her madness."

Marcel Monnier was asked how it happened that Madame Marcel Monnier never saw her sister-in-law again after the period of her marriage (1874). "And how is it that your daughter has never seen her aunt?"

A: "Moral reasoning made my mother decide to prevent her daughter-in-law and her granddaughter from seeing my sister. She would use very foul language. To a certain degree, I shared my mother's feelings and did not insist."

Questioned in turn, Marie-Dolorès Monnier, Marcel Monnier's daughter, said: "Twice a week I went to my grandmother's, on Thursday and Sunday, around three o'clock; often I wasn't let in; when I was admitted to see her, the conversation ran out quickly, as she only spoke to me about the difficulties she was having with the servants and her illnesses; not accustomed to being cosseted by her, I was paralyzed in her presence and I didn't say much; the conversation would last around a half-hour and I would leave after asking, if I thought of it, for news of my aunt Blanche. My grandmother always replied: 'She's fine.'"

Now let's hear Madame Monnier, the mother.

"Never did I think of confining my daughter, whom I loved so much. She was always free to move about the house, but I must say that for the past twenty-five years, she has voluntarily retreated to her room; I might even add to her bed, for I believe that since 1876, and even perhaps before, she has insisted on staying in bed, despite the efforts of myself and my husband to have her get some fresh air.

"She always had very delicate health. . . . Nevertheless, she managed to do her schoolwork. She loved work, and above all reading. . . .

"As a young girl, she rarely had a social life. . . . She preferred above all to go to churches, and I thought that she had the vocation to become a nun.

"There was never any question of her planning to marry. Moreover, I am convinced that she never would have wanted to marry.

"In 1872, I believe, my daughter was afflicted with a very serious pernicious fever that threatened her life. Since then, she has not wished to see anyone. However, she went to Mont-de-Marsan for the marriage of her brother, whom she loves very much. Shortly after she returned to Poitiers, she was constantly staying shut up in her room; she refused to put clothes on, on the pretext that she was so weak that she didn't have the strength to wear them. She ate very little and was already extremely thin.

"She wasn't at all mad, but she had very odd ways of doing things. She didn't want to sleep with sheets; she refused to wear a nightdress. . . . She was only happy when she was entirely covered by a blanket. . . .

"It's been several years already since the doctor came to see her, because she hasn't been sick."

When the condition in which her daughter was found is described to her, she replies that for the past three months she was ill and unable to visit her any more. Previously, she went up twice a day; she had seen all the filth, but Blanche had not wanted it to be touched.

Q: "The servants often asked you to have the bed changed and to let your daughter be washed. You always refused."

A: "They are liars. They are two hussies."

. . . .

A: "If I made a mistake, it wasn't with the intention of killing my daughter. I always sacrificed myself for her."

Madame Monnier was imprisoned on May 24, 1901, around six o'clock in the evening. She was immediately placed in the infirmary.

She seemed very ill but kept her appetite and did not complain too much. On June 6 her condition started to worsen. She proclaimed her innocence and asked to be allowed to leave, arguing that her son had already left the prison, and several times, despite her weakness and her prostrate condition, she busied herself making bundles of her things. The night of the seventh was very arduous. At five o'clock in the morning the sick woman asked for something to drink. Realizing that death was near, the nurse who stayed with her alerted the warden, who had the chaplain and doctor called. The latter arrived in time for the death agony. He made futile attempts to revive Madame Monnier, who died very quietly at 9:30. A few minutes before the doctor arrived, Madame Monnier cried out, "Ah, my poor Blanche!"

Chapter 3

On May 23, 1901, around seven o'clock in the evening, Blanche Monnier arrived at the Poitiers hospital.

I have in front of me a large photograph taken immediately after she entered the hospital, a photograph that was reproduced by the great illustrated periodicals of the day. It is impossible to imagine anything more striking than this poor girl's glance and her smile—for she was smiling, an angelic, idyllic smile, but somehow crafty, as if mocking.

She was in a horribly dirty condition, witnesses of the time tell us. Her face, as pale as wax, was highly emaciated. A thick layer of filth covered areas of her extremely thin body. The nails on her hands and feet were very long.

Her hair formed a dense mass more than a meter in length, thirty centimeters wide, and four to five centimeters thick. It was a thick matting, made up of hair mixed with excremental matter and scraps of food. The odor given off by this mass was so ghastly that doctors authorized the people present to smoke cigarettes. This mass of hair was all on the left side, with the right side of the head presenting only a few tufts, diminished by continual rubbing and worn away due to the position that Blanche Monnier had held during the entire time that she had remained stretched out on her mallet, lying on her right side, curled up.

Blanche Monnier's total weight when she entered the hospital was fifty-six pounds. It was astonishing that the poor girl could have lived for so many years in such squalid destitution, in a dark atmosphere, so pestilential that it made everyone recoil. Her state of weakness when she entered the hospital was such that the chaplain, fearing an imminent death, felt it necessary to administer the sacrament of extreme unction immediately. By the next day, however, Blanche Monnier began to be noticeably better. She gladly accepted the food that was brought to her. Her organs were judged to be perfectly healthy by the doctors called into consultation.

Blanche Monnier replied fairly well to some simple and precise questions; she identified flowers that were given to her and recalled some memories of her youth, particularly an estate that her family owned at

Migné.[6] But quite often she refused to reply, sending those who spoke to her packing by exclaiming curses and insults. If one still persisted in trying to get an answer from her, she quickly became enraged and changed from her usual immobility to a state of fierce agitation. Her general weakness prevented her from turning violent, however, and hiding her face in her pillow, she merely muttered unintelligible words and phrases with no discernible meaning, mixed with numerous oaths.

An obsession almost always returned when she was vexed: she wanted to return to her former home, which she named with an unintelligible phrase: "her dear good back-mill-in-piâtre."[7]

Already, when they came to get her at the rue de la Visitation to remove her from her hovel, she clung to her straw mattress and putrid blanket, pleading to be allowed to live tranquilly in her dear little cave.

As the reports stated, "She never asked the least question about any subject and never spoke of the people whom she usually saw in her home. Most of the time, she agreed to respond only to those people who took care of her every day and brought her meals.

"All her responses were absolutely childish. She could identify most of the objects that were brought to her, pencils, roses, drinking glasses, and food items, and always called them her dear little pencil, dear little rose, and so on. She even often called for her 'dear little cloth,' with which she had covered her head during her time at the house and which was covered with filth and insects.

"In any case, she hadn't the least notion of hygiene and always relieved herself in her bed or in the clothes she had been given to wear. On June 18, however, she began to accept using a chamber pot for urinating.

"She could be urged to write her first name and a few words with a pencil or pen. Her handwriting was fairly clear, but after a well-written word would come shapeless scribblings.

"Her appetite was excellent. She greedily ate the food that was of-

6. Tr. note: Migné-Auxances, a small town located six kilometers north of Poitiers, is noted for a seventeenth-century religious community, Le Carmel de l'Incarnation, and a miraculous appearance of a glowing cross said to have occurred in 1826.

7. Tr. note: Blanche's exact words are "moulin en piâtre." The word *piâtre* is not a noun in French, although it sounds like the monetary term *piastre* and the word for plaster, *plâtre*

fered to her. Her meals are very copious." (In fact, successive weighings indicated a rapid augmentation, from 25.5 kilos on May 25 to 35.5 kilos on August 3.)

Her physical energy grew proportionately, but her mental faculties were far from following this progressive advance. It's true that Blanche answered certain questions a bit better, but she still remained indifferent to external things and never asked questions.

Father de Mondion, the hospital's chaplain, came to speak with her several times. He asked her whether she remembered her first communion. Blanche Monnier responded affirmatively and could even repeat to him the names of the priests who gave her religious instruction. She also recalled the names of the family's former food suppliers, saying that she bought candies not at Avenel's, the confectioner, but from Pasino, an Italian. She recognized and named all the flowers given to her in the numerous bouquets that charitable souls brought to her each day. Nothing gave her more pleasure, adds the priest, than to see and smell the flowers. She is delighted to glimpse the countryside from her bed and expresses her joy by shouting, "Oh, how lovely it is!" When swallows fly over, she recognizes them perfectly and shouts, "Oh! Look there, the nice little swallows."

She was extremely gentle, listened to what she was told, did as everyone one asked her to, and kept her underwear on without trying to remove it, so that only one nurse was required to keep an eye on her. When she was left alone, which occurred fairly often, she created no mess. But when the priest asked her whether she wanted to see her brother and mother again, Blanche immediately replied: "Oh, don't bring them here!" When on another occasion he asked whether she was comfortable at home, Blanche exclaimed: "Don't let's talk about that, it's a house that puts everything on the run, everything on the run."

I need not emphasize the extraordinary inconsistency of Blanche Monnier's replies. The reader will observe them for himself. The effort, unconscious or not, by which we seek during questioning to reduce the inconsistencies, to make a prisoner agree with himself, is always useless, and particularly so in the case of Blanche Monnier, who seemed to rejoice at the clean air that she could finally breathe, the cleanliness of her hospital bed, and all the care from which she was benefiting, while at the same time missing her filthy bed and the noxious darkness of her "dear little grotto," of which she spoke in tender terms, which seemed to become in her mind a sort of mythic place that she named in such an odd way that it took a while at first to understand what she meant when she said and repeated: "I'd like to go back into *my dear great-Back-Malampia*"[8]—where it seems, moreover, that she had not been as badly treated as was feared at first, for when she was served chicken in the hospital, she said: "I also got some in my dear great-Back-Malampia."

"I witnessed Mademoiselle Monnier's meals several times," an intern told us. "Her first statement, before touching what was given her: 'How clean it is.' She still ate with her fingers, *but with much delicacy.*"

And the hospital bursar reported: "When she ate an orange, she knew how to keep the seeds in the hollow of her hand until someone took them away."

It seems to me that she sought, at least unconsciously, to be in harmony with the people who came to see her and question her or gave in to a sort of instinctive sympathy. That's what allowed Sister Saint-Wilfred, a nun at the hospital, to say that far from being afraid of cleanliness, Blanche took pleasure in being washed, sleeping between fresh white sheets, and having a nightshirt on her. She said nothing while her hair was being cut, a process that the felting of her head of hair made especially hard. She was pleased, immediately thereafter, to let her head be bathed in a special perfumed water.

"Far from loving bad odors," said Sister Saint-Wilfred, "she enjoyed the aroma of flowers and eau de cologne that was sprinkled over her entire body and her bed. When she saw a rosy-colored morning sky, she showed great joy. In general, everything that was very bright pleased her; on the contrary, she detested everything of a dark color. Thus she didn't want to accept letters with black borders and refused to keep a ring that an intern jokingly put on her finger because the ring had a black stone as a setting. She was very glad to get dressed again each morning. She easily accepted wearing slippers. It was necessary to insist that she put on stockings, but I must add that the difficulty was

8. Tr. note: Gide accepts that Blanche's speech is often idiosyncratic and unintelligible.

easily overcome. Once dressed, she looked at herself with satisfaction and above all looked at the rows of braid that decorated her dressing gown. Her joy was great. She said: 'It's too lovely for this house. It would go much better in the dear fine house in great-Back-Malampia.'"

Here the worthy nun added: "No doubt Blanche Monnier was alluding to a family estate, for she often spoke to us about Migné." But we think that Blanche meant by these words, as we have stated, her filthy room, or at least the extraordinary transposition that was made of the room within her mind.

"Once settled into an armchair near the window," Sister Saint-Wilfred continued, "Blanche looked at the countryside, while saying, as she had on previous days, 'How lovely it is'; she would point out to the guard and myself when swallows went by, mentioning their name. . . . She showed the same visible pleasure when contemplating, at length and closely, the pictures and flowers brought to her, making it clear that Mademoiselle Monnier had long been deprived of such sights.

"The bed occupied by Mademoiselle Monnier was placed facing the window. As soon as Mademoiselle Monnier arrived, the casement was put wide open, letting light and air penetrate into the room. I observed that, during the first moments, she wanted to hide her face under the blanket. It's probable that the bright light tired her eyes, for starting the next day, she no longer tried to hide her face entirely; she only raised the sheet with her left hand to the level of her eyes. She still continues this odd habit, although quite often her face is completely uncovered, above all when she eats her meals; not a single time has she asked (and she knows very well how to ask for what she pleases) that the window or the shutters be closed."

Long accustomed to relieving herself in the sheets, it was rather difficult to get her to change her habits. Her nurse, Amélie Raymond, nevertheless stated on June 22, that "since last week Mademoiselle Monnier has made more progress, and she has become cleaner and cleaner. During the day she asks me for the chamber pot and knows quite well how to wait when I am busy."

The hospital intern confirmed the witnesses' testimony and added: "Like all the other people who listened to her, I observed that she often spoke provincial dialect and she used very foul expressions. At first Mademoiselle Monnier seemed in a state of collapse, and her answers were often incomprehensible; she had difficulty in explaining her thoughts; in the last three or four days, however [this was said on June 8] a noteworthy change has occurred; she knows quite well how to ask for what she wants to eat at meals. This morning she told me she wanted to eat 'some dear little chicken, some dear little brocs (strawberries), and a dear little chocolate macaroon!' I wrote the menu down on my notepad, and she read it very ably.

"I should point out, if you haven't already been told, that Mademoiselle Monnier usually prefaces each word with 'the dear little'; she is starting to use swear words a bit less often."

She ate with pleasure the orange segments given to her by the intern on duty. Her pleasure was even greater when one of the nurses who usually tended her gave her a bouquet made of different flowers. Then she looked for a long time, inhaled deeply, and as a child might do, kissed the bouquet and the hand that had brought it. She would say at such moments in a slightly rapid voice: "Oh, how lovely it would be to have two bouquets like that with a grotto in between and a little Virgin Mary in the grotto. We must do that another time."

She was haunted by the image of a grotto, connected in her mind with the memory of her room on the rue de la Visitation and perhaps some indefinable mystical notion.

Madame Monnier, her mother, died on the night of June 7, as we have said. The mother superior of the hospital thought that she herself should announce this bereavement to Blanche Monnier.

"I have sad news to tell you, Mademoiselle Blanche," she said to her. "Your mother is dead."

"I want a party. I want a party," the patient replied simply, with a covetous glance at her meal (according to the *Journal de l'ouest* of June 11).

"But Mademoiselle Blanche, listen to me carefully," continued the mother superior in a tone of infinite sweetness. "When you go back home, you won't find your mother there any more."

"Peuh! Peuh! I want a party! I want a party!"

Her reply was always the same, whether one spoke to Mademoiselle Blanche of the mourning clothes that she had to wear or described the grief that her brother Marcel might be feeling.

On July 17 Blanche Monnier replied to the questions asked of her in this way:

Q: "Will you answer the questions I'm going to ask you?"

A: "I don't want to answer anything at all."

Q: "Did you have some visitors yesterday?"

A: "A few ladies with pretty dresses for me to look at."

Q: "Did you go walking in the garden and did you feel strong enough to go?"

A: "No, I didn't go. I might go out later to take a walk in the little garden of the dear good-great-Back and at Migné [the Monnier family estate, le Pilet, is located at mischievous]."

Q: "Do you remember Juliette Dupuis or Eugénie Tabeau?"

A: "I don't know what's become of them; too bad for them."

Q: "Do you know Carcassonnne and Montpellier?"

A: "All that is much too far away."

Q: "Do you remember your room at 'dear good-great-Back'?"

A: (Mademoiselle Monnier makes inarticulate noises, and it's impossible to understand what she is saying. She seems angry.)

Q: "Did your brother sometimes read the newspaper to you?"

A: "He mustn't come here; he's fine where he is."

Q: "Don't you want to see your brother?"

Mademoiselle Monnier replies very angrily: "Let him stay where he is; he's just fine."

As her reply is being dictated, at the word *angrily,* Mademoiselle Monnier says, "That's a sin, one mustn't get involved with it."

Q: "Would you be pleased to see Madame Marcel Monnier?"

A: "I don't know what's become of her. Let her stay where she is."

Q: "Would you like to see Mademoiselle Dolorès Monnier, your niece?"

A: "I don't know what's become of her. Too bad for her; too bad for everybody."

Q: "Do you know Marie Fazy?"

A: "I don't know what's become of her."

Q: "Didn't you know that she is dead?"

Mademoiselle Monnier says a certain number of unintelligible phrases. She seems tired now.

From the physical point of view, her progress continues to be rapid, but her reason has not returned.

"She is not in possession of her faculties; she says eccentric and discontinuous things; we have diagnosed feeblemindedness. She is insane, there's no doubt about it," declares Dr. Lagrange, a psychiatrist at Poitiers. By contrast, Father Mondion, the "very kind hospital chaplain" from Poitiers, objects to this label of madness: "I find it disturbing," he wrote in the *Journal de l'ouest* on June 5, "that in the religious party there are persons to be found who would wish to excuse or justify this crime; I feel that on the contrary, we must completely separate the religious and conservative party from this case. I would also like to point out one matter: as a means of justifying the guilty persons, it's said that Mademoiselle Blanche is insane and that she had a passion for taking off her clothing. She has been with us for nine days, and we've noticed that she has a passion for covering herself up. If one approaches her too closely, she shrinks away and pulls the covers over her. Thus, she has a sense of modesty. . . . In short, we would be much better off letting the court decide rather than trying to justify a dreadful crime. . . . I've said, and I repeat, that those who leave an unknown woman, a daughter, or a sister in the pitiful state in which Mademoiselle Blanche was when she entered the hospital are criminals, all the more because the victim is gentle, calm, and well-behaved. Her windows are not kept shut, and she has never given the least sign of malicious or dangerous madness. . . . That she should be in a state of mental and physical depression is hardly surprising, given that she remained for so many years without air or light and almost without food."

We will attempt to understand a bit better who these "criminals" were, this mother and brother who are otherwise presented as such honorable people. What were the motives of their crime? What I find particularly interesting about this case is that, as we come to know the circumstances better, the mystery deepens, leaves the domain of the facts, and nestles within the personality of the victim as much as in the personalities of the accused. We will try to shed sufficient light on these accused with the use of testimony from several witnesses. Madame Monnier and her son, in fact, felt themselves to be totally innocent, and we will see that the court ultimately agreed with them. Before introducing the mother Madame Monnier and her son in a more intimate way, let's devote a few words to their forebears.

Chapter 4

The large, well-produced, and highly interesting pamphlet *Remarks in Favor of Monsieur Marcel Monnier,* written to clear him, was handed out at the courthouse door on the day of the hearing. I call attention to the following facts it cites about different members of his family:

The mother, Madame Monnier, was born in November 28, 1825, in Poitiers, where her father, Monsieur Demarconnay, had a modest stockbroker's practice.

Her maternal grandfather was a process server in the same city, and the stockbroker's brother worked at the same profession in Vouillé.[9]

The elder Monsieur Monnier was teaching rhetoric at the Poitiers high school when he married Mademoiselle Demarconnay, on July 8, 1846. Later he became a professor of humanities and the dean of the faculty in the same city.

It seems probable that Madame Monnier assumed all authority in the family, and her husband had to resign himself to it, since everyone describes her as imperiously imposing her yoke.

Monsieur and Madame Monnier had two children: Marcel, born on February 27, 1848, and Blanche, born March 1, 1849.

Monsieur and Madame Monnier lived in Poitiers in a house situated on the rue de la Visitation that belonged to Monsieur Demarconnay, her father.

9. Tr. note: Vouillé, a small town in the Poitou-Charentes region, was home of the legend of Mélusine.

Monsieur Demarconnay, retired from his career, also lived there along with his children until his death.

Monsieur Monnier the elder died there on April 9, 1882.

Monsieur Demarconnay died there in turn one year later, on April 21, 1883.

Madame Demarconnay, née Kleiber, had preceded him into the grave ten years before.

Among the witnesses who testified, the only one who stated that he had visited Monsieur Demarconnay said in very expressive terms that his daughter's and granddaughter's eccentricity and lunacy ran in the family, as he was "quite a character and very hotheaded" (Father Montbron's testimony).

Without being infirm, Monsieur Demarconnay spent the last part of his life in total seclusion, locking himself in his room on the third floor, from which he did not emerge, not even to be present for the last moments of his son-in-law, who died in another room on the same landing.

No one ever saw him in the street during his last ten years.

The former servants confirmed this voluntary seclusion. One of them, a woman named Gault, added that "not being specially ordered to take care of this new hermit, who never left his room," she left the house after working there for three or four months without having ever glimpsed him. Only by hearsay did she know of his existence.

Chapter 5

Madame Monnier was seventy-five years old at the time of her arrest (she looked no older than sixty-five or even sixty-two, according to certain witnesses). She was a small woman, rather heavy, with hard features, who most often appeared with her head covered by a black bonnet trimmed with lace and ribbons. She led a secluded life, receiving almost no visitors, and went out more and more rarely to the city, where she was esteemed and respected but not loved. The extensive testimony that was gathered agreed on this point: "Her personality was authoritarian and irritable." Madame R. C., the wife of a teacher in

Poitiers who had been a friend of Monsieur Monnier, one of the few people she would agree to see, tells us the following: In the month of April 1882, when the elder Monsieur Monnier died, Madame Monnier, who could not stand being accompanied to the funeral by her daughter-in-law, whom she loathed, sent for her to be present during the sad ceremony. From this day forth Madame Monnier became accustomed to Madame R. C.'s calling on her fairly regularly, around once a week, preferably on Saturday, at three o'clock, after her doctor's visit(?). "That way," said Madame Monnier, "I had to dress up only once a week, and I could wear a dressing gown on the other days." These weekly visits continued for ten years. Madame Monnier had no callers apart from Madame R. C. and a cousin, Madame Halleau, whose visits were far less frequent.

Madame R. C. informs us that Madame Monnier often spoke of her daughter, Blanche. To her knowledge Blanche never intended to marry but rather sought to take her vows; she was dissuaded by Dr. Guérineau and the hospital's mother superior. Madame R. C. often advised Madame Monnier to go back to living with her daughter in the large main portion of her house. The two of them might have had adjoining rooms there, and Blanche would have been better tended. But Madame Monnier refused this change, which, she said, would have been too hard for the servants. "Madame Monnier never asked me if I wanted to see her daughter," said Madame R. C. "One day I wrote to her offering to send one of my daughters to keep her company; I understood from her silence that she didn't want anyone to be in communication with Mademoiselle Blanche, and I didn't insist."

Monsieur Marcel Monnier often had violent discussions with his mother. She had forbidden him to visit her estate, located at Migné, and when she learned that he went there anyway, despite her interdiction, she furiously hurled abuse at him and threw him out. On another day Marcel Monnier picked a flower from the garden of his mother, whom he had come to visit, and a truly scandalous scene between them resulted; they almost wound up striking each other. Once again Madame Monnier threw out her son and forbade the servants to let him in if he ever came back. But most of their scenes were about the subject of money. Madame Monnier paid her son an allowance, and there were always difficulties between them each time the sum came due. One particular day Madame R. C. found her in an extremely angry mood: "I insist on being the master in my own house," she told her. "I've just thrown my son out, and forbidden him ever to return." Madame R. C. immediately added that this scene, which at first she thought was about a financial matter, could well have been about Blanche, for Madame Monnier complained that her son insisted that his sister be sent to a nursing home, a suggestion that she refused to carry out and would always reject. She had made a will, she said, above all to prevent her son from changing an arrangement of which she approved. Her daughter, for whom she had always sacrificed herself, must continue to live in the room that she had already occupied for several years and of which a specific clause in Madame Monnier's will left her the ownership, along with the right to stay on, even after her mother's death.[10]

Madame R. C. hinted that perhaps fear of being deprived of the 5,000 franc annuity that his mother gave him kept Monsieur Marcel Monnier from opposing her decisions and led him to close his eyes to a situation of which he disapproved.

Then suddenly, without any explanation, Madame Monnier closed her door to Madame R. C., although apparently without being particularly ill-disposed to her, for she included her in her 1885 will, which she could have easily changed. Therefore, this should be seen only as an aggravation of her surly temperament and habit of shunning all social activities. We are informed by Monsieur F. C., honorary secretary of the law school, that for many years Madame Monnier gave orders that no one should enter her home. The large front door was always locked, and

---

10.   Last Will and Testament of Madame Monnier.

In her will dated January 5, 1885, Madame Monnier *disinherited her son* as far as the law allowed.

Out of a fortune of 500,000 francs at most, she bequeathed to persons outside the family 151,700 francs (to which must be added 25,000 francs in costs).

Moreover, for her daughter, she declared:

"I will and bequeath to . . . my daughter . . . the usufruct and possession, during her lifetime, *of the room she currently inhabits,* of the one she previously inhabited, of the room facing the former, and my father's office . . .

"*I insist that my daughter continue to reside, after my demise, in the part of the house of which I have just bequeathed her the usufruct.*

"I wish that all my daughter's assets, including those she may acquire later, be spent only for the care she requires."

it was necessary to go through a small courtyard to get into the house. During Monsieur Monnier's lifetime, it was still possible to visit the house, but after the head of the family died, strict instructions must have been given, for no one except for serving maids went in anymore. We therefore must rely on the testimony of these women, who were replaced quite often, to try to understand what happened inside the strange house where, one of them told us, "we always seemed to be walking on tiptoe." But their testimony could not be taken at face value, above all for matters dealing with the confined woman's nourishment. It isn't perfectly clear, indeed, that Blanche Monnier herself enjoyed the oysters and chicken that her mother had served to her (as bills from the food suppliers attest). These refined meals do not correspond well to the sordid miserliness for which Madame Monnier would later be reproached. But Madame Monnier, the servants tell us, never entered her daughter's room and could not know whether the chickens and oysters that she bought were reaching the confined woman. Yet Blanche Monnier, once she was in the hospital, spoke of the chickens served to her at dear good great-Back-Malampia. This is one of the points of this strange story that remains the most difficult to clarify and where the inconsistency of characters is especially disturbing, for in other respects—and here all the ancillary testimony agrees—Madame Monnier stubbornly refused to allow the sheets, blanket, or mattress of her daughter's bed to be changed, even though she had a sizable supply of them in other rooms in the house: "Madame Monnier was a filthy miser, to the point where I didn't dare ask her for my pay myself; I was forced to have my mother ask for it," we are told by Alcide Texier, a ticket-taker at the United Bus Company who had worked as a servant for Madame Monnier when he was only seventeen years old. "During the six months that I spent in the house, I always saw her wearing the same badly soiled dress."

It truly seems that all the members of this family possessed a love of dirt more than true miserliness. We will see this odd taste appear in the son in an even more repulsive manner. But perhaps it is a matter of miserliness in the following statement by Juliette Dupuis: "In the evenings Mademoiselle Monnier ate almost nothing; just a brioche or a cake called a jésuite; and in the morning, for her breakfast at nine o'clock, nothing but a cup of hot chocolate from the Compagnie Coloniale, as Miss Monnier didn't want any bread. By contrast, the midday meal, which it was my duty to bring to Mademoiselle Blanche, generally consisted of a fried sole and a cutlet surrounded by potatoes; the meal was prepared by a girl called Tabeau. Sometimes we sent out to the Hôtel de France and, before that, to the Hôtel de l'Europe (the hotel bills prove this), either for a chicken with cream sauce and mushrooms or chicken à la rousse. Often there were oysters,[11] when they were in season, and also pâté de foie gras." Monsieur Robin, owner of the Hôtel de France, confirmed that dishes were ordered from him in this manner, often two or three times per week.

A bill from the Maillard-Laurendeau establishment given to the examining magistrate mentioned a relatively high amount of the best-quality table wine at o francs, 75 per bottle, and of fine Bordeaux wine at 2 francs and 3 francs per bottle, provided during the last two years for Madame Monnier, whose habits of sobriety and extreme thriftiness do not permit us to suppose that she spent this amount for herself.

Madame Monnier's ordinary menu was highly simple. It does not appear that she touched the oysters, chickens, or foie gras that were brought for her daughter.

Next we shall read the testimony of the maid Dupuis:

"I brought her food on a plate, never adding a knife because I knew she didn't want one. She claimed that a pious girl must never use a knife. There was always a fork on the plate, but no spoon because she never ate soup. In any case, Mademoiselle Monnier didn't want to use the fork; she ate with her hands. I didn't bring any napkins, even though Mademoiselle Monnier sometimes asked me for them to wipe 'her little handies,' because Madame Monnier refused to give me any." Another servant informs us that Mademoiselle Monnier didn't always eat the food brought to her right away but put aside, on her straw mattress next to her, a portion of her meal—which would explain the amount of rubbish. "Sometimes Monsieur Marcel Monnier came when I was feeding his sister; he was never involved with her food and never tried to see if she needed

11. Madame Fort, an oyster vendor, testified: "For twenty-five years I sold oysters to the Monnier family. Their maids came to buy them every day or so. Madame Monnier required the finest and freshest ones for Mademoiselle Blanche."

anything. At lunchtime Mademoiselle Monnier drank white wine, cut with water. She was never refused food or drink that I know of."

Let's interrupt Juliette Dupuis's testimony for a moment to insert this astounding excerpt from Virginie Neveux's testimony, from which I will later quote other equally sensational parts:

"Blanche Monnier ate the same food as her mother, but to drink Madame Monnier had her only given sugar water in which she dissolved ether. It often happened that Blanche refused to drink it; then the mother had us bring the glass holding this drink down to the cellar, and every day we'd offer it to her again, until she drank it."

"When I got there in 1899"—Juliette Dupuis continued—"Mademoiselle Monnier's room was in the condition you saw, the same furniture, same bedding, same filthiness. We, the Tabeau girl and I, often asked Madame Monnier for replacements for the sheets, blankets, a bolster, a mattress; we met with a total refusal: Madame Monnier replied that we would never manage to keep her clean. I must state, however, that it would have been easy for us, the Tabeau girl and myself, to wash her and accustom her to clean habits; when we saw that Madame Monnier absolutely wanted her daughter to sleep on a pallet full of vermin, naked, with no nightdress, covered only by a dirty blanket, and when we noted that we were forbidden to open the window whose shutters had been padlocked and we were forced to keep the door closed on the pretext that Mademoiselle Monnier might catch cold, we said no more about it; but we notified the neighbors.

"There was a foul odor in Mademoiselle Monnier's room, and the air wasn't breathable, which was not surprising, for this young lady did her excrements in bed, and we were allowed to remove the little undersheet folded into quarters only in the evening, at nine-thirty.

"Madame Monnier knew perfectly well what a horrible state of filth her daughter was left in. All she said was: 'Ah, poor child, what do you expect me to do about it?'

"Monsieur Monnier was aware of everything. He came very often to see his sister and never asked us to keep her clean; on the contrary, when we wanted to let air into the room through the door only, for the window was always tightly sealed, he went to alert his mother, who reproached us harshly."

The testimony of Madame Monnier's servants is, as I've noted, often contradictory. To try to gather and organize them in summary form would be to distort and remove a large part of their interest. Each one has its own personality, and it seems to me that the best is to set down the most outstanding excerpts here.

Let's hear from Juliette Brault, whom Madame Monnier employed first as a chambermaid and then as cook, from June 1897 until September 1898:

"The first time that I went into Mademoiselle Monnier's room, I shuddered; the odor that came from Mademoiselle Monnier's bed was foul. At that time there were no scraps of meat or excrement, but the straw mattress and bedding were completely rotted, as Mademoiselle Perroche, who was a servant with me, must have told you. Mademoiselle Monnier was completely naked, wrapped in a dirty blanket, and I observed that very often cockroaches ran over her; every evening a sheet folded into quarters was placed under Mademoiselle Monnier; it was intended to catch her excrements, and it was only changed every twenty-four hours.

"Mademoiselle Monnier wasn't absolutely mad; sometimes she said sensible things, but she didn't want to be washed and always kept her head covered. The furniture was covered with a thick layer of dust that was impossible to remove, because the casement and shutters were never opened; sometimes I let air in through the door, despite strict orders from Madame Monnier, who wanted all openings to be tightly sealed; during severe heat waves, however, she allowed the door to be opened.

"For fifteen months I slept in this room; the odor was unbearable, although it was almost tolerable when the door was open, so I always left the door open at night. If Madame Monnier had known, she would have been angry, because she would have said that we wanted to make her daughter catch cold. I asked very often, as did Hélène Bonneau and Berthe Perroche, who were servants at the same time as myself, to change the straw mattress and bedding; we always met with a total refusal from Madame Monnier, who told us: 'You may not change it. Ah, the poor girl, how she has ruined me!' I must state that there were straw mattresses and bedding in the house that weren't being used; it wouldn't have been necessary to buy any. When I spoke about a night-dress to Madame Monnier, she replied: 'The poor child, she doesn't want any.'

"Mademoiselle Monnier had no underclothes, and the dresser in her room had no drawers.

"I swear that if they wanted us to, we could have kept Mademoiselle Monnier clean; but then other helpers would have been needed, as well as a wish to do so, which did not exist either in Madame or in Monsieur Monnier her son.

"I never saw Mademoiselle Monnier out of bed. Several times I tried to see her face, but I never could; her body was appallingly thin, even though she was properly fed; in the morning she was served coffee with milk or hot chocolate, at noontime at least two dishes, and in the evening she didn't want anything.

"I left Madame Monnier because I couldn't get along any more with a woman who was so miserly and authoritarian.

"I felt sorry for Mademoiselle Blanche Monnier with all my heart, but didn't think of alerting the law."

Mademoiselle Blanche would remain leaning on her elbow, maintaining a very uncomfortable position, we were told by Louise Quinqueneau, née Pichard. "It would have been easy to put a bolster and a pillow under her head, but they would have had to be replaced from time to time, and that's what Madame Monnier didn't want. The woman's miserliness was such that despite my complaints and the insistence of the servants who were with me, it was impossible to obtain a change of bedding, which was in a dreadful condition. One day, however, I begged Madame Monnier so much that she permitted me to get a mattress from a room in the main portion of the house. This part of the home had many complete beds that went unused; I took the mattress down to Mademoiselle Blanche's room; when Madame Monnier saw that we were going to use it to replace the bed with rotted feathers, she forbade this change, and I had to bring the mattress back again.

"I remember that a few days before I left, I had an argument with Madame Monnier because she always wanted to use the same sheets and linen, even though her linen cupboards were full.

"I often criticized Madame Monnier for leaving her daughter in such a filthy condition, and I encouraged her to hire a nurse; she replied that there was no point, because her daughter wasn't sick and that anyway she was fine as she was, because she always seemed happy."

"Not only did Mademoiselle Blanche live that way," another servant informs us, "but she enjoyed it very much. I remember having asked her one day if she wouldn't be happy to be in a nice clean room, pretty, and decorated with fine furniture. She told me: 'Oh, my dear little grotto! I wouldn't want to leave it for a moment for anything in the world. I'm just fine here.'

"At one point," Berthe Perroche tells us, "the straw mattress and bedding were so rotted that we asked to replace them with other, damaged ones that were in the house. Madame Monnier refused and told us that we were not allowed to give them to her and that anyway, she did not want them to be ruined. But she did allow us, after countless hesitations, to make three little cushions ourselves; we put one underneath the young lady; the other two were saved as replacement cushions.

"We asked Madame Monnier to have her daughter sent to a nursing home, and she replied that she had vowed to stay with her daughter until her death."

Let's hear Juliette Dupuis again: "Monsieur Marcel Monnier cannot say that he didn't see the filth in which his sister was left, because I swear that at least once in my presence, and in front of Eugénie Tabeau, he watched, with his mother at his side, what we called *putting Mademoiselle Blanche to bed,* which consisted of the following: the young lady rose up on all fours; the cook lifted up the blankets that Mademoiselle Blanche was wrapped in, except the one covering her head, and then she took out the sheet folded into quarters that contained the excrement from the past twenty-four hours and also took out a small cushion made of oat husks that was absolutely disgusting; a dry, although very dirty, cushion was replaced on the bed with another sheet, rinsed out but never scrubbed, and Mademoiselle Monnier went back to her former position.

"Monsieur Marcel Monnier having watched this scene at least once, it would be wrong for him to insist that he believed that his sister was well taken care of; the small cushion made of oat husks dried out all winter in the room; he couldn't have avoided seeing it."

How can the brother's peculiar behavior be explained? It's time to speak a little about him.

The excellent pamphlet by Monsieur Barbier, a lawyer at the appellate court and former leader of the bar, from which we have already borrowed some material, will enlighten us once more.

Chapter 6

A photograph of Marcel Monnier that we have before us shows him wearing a short felt top hat with a rather wide brim. His head is sunken between his shoulders; a stiff little black tie can be seen, but not his collar. The lines going from the corners of his lips to the wings of his nose are deeply etched. A drooping mustache, very thick, joins the heavy sideburns that extend underneath his very wide, clean-shaven chin. He wears a pince-nez. His myopic gaze is oddly sidelong and veiled.

We've seen that Marcel Monnier, possessing a very weak character, let himself be entirely dominated by his mother. She had never stopped "treating him like a little boy." He was sometimes able to strike back, however, as is shown in a letter to his mother dated June 11, 1893, reproduced in Monsieur Barbier's report:

"Before taking the extreme measures that I will be forced to adopt to meet my social standing, I wish to inform you once again that I absolutely need 2,500 francs in order to live in Poitiers. You owe me those 2,500 francs, seeing that my grandfather's formal wish was always that my allowance be continued after his death. I will call as witnesses several people who heard him say it. This is also proven by letters I received from him, which I have taken care to keep in my drawer.

"Simple good sense alone shows that we cannot live on the 1,230 francs that you gave me yesterday (for twenty francs were missing, so you didn't even give us 1,250 francs). *You didn't give us a cent as a New Year's gift* this year, and despite all the expenses I've had in maintaining my social standing at a time when more than ever we must show that we are not a family of poor wretches, I have never asked you for so much as a centime. It seems to me that rather than accuse us of being spendthrifts, you should praise and thank us for having brought your granddaughter into the world and having succeeded in giving her a warm welcome.

"You who seem to think so much about the wine I drink, I must inform you that starting from today, I will only drink water and eat beans.

"Rather than lose our social standing, we will deprive ourselves of food, and this winter we will not have a scrap of fire in the house. . . . In any case, there's no point in making us leave the rue de Boncenne just to take away with one hand twice as much as you gave us with the other.

"You can pride yourself on cutting my life short, *and if I should be buried soon, we'll know who to blame.*"

Witnesses abound who describe him as "equally myopic morally and visually" and "of an unbelievable naïveté." He wasn't exactly unintelligent. His friends, who included the pianist Francis Planté,[12] whom he often saw from the time when he was prefectural councilor at Mont-de-Marsan, liked him and were amused by his eccentricities. He was not uncultured, even having some literary pretensions, about which, moreover, only a few close friends knew. They admitted that he "rebelled against the simplest attention to and practices of cleanliness." He was anxious to make his bed himself, we are told by Mademoiselle Giraud, who was his chambermaid for some time. Another chambermaid, Mademoiselle Godard, informs us that he never wanted his bedsheets to be changed. "It had to be done without his noticing, and when he saw that it had been done, it made him angry." He put a small box at the head of his bed to serve as a bolster. He kept his room from being cleaned. It was dirty and disgusting, never swept out; all the objects in it were covered by a thick layer of dust, everything was in the greatest disarray, and several half-filled slop pails were always to be found. Should we see in this nothing more than "negligence," a word used by some of the witnesses? It seems instead, as we shall shortly see, that Marcel Monnier enjoyed being in filth. Even the word *filth* isn't strong enough. And one is less surprised that Monsieur Marcel Monnier was not dis-

---

12. Tr. note: Francis Planté, an eminent French piano virtuoso (1839–1934), was a friend and colleague of Rossini, Liszt, Mendelssohn, and Gounod. He often played duo recitals with Camille Saint-Saëns.

turbed by the foul odor of his sister's straw mattress and hair but, on the contrary, enjoyed it when one learns the following:

A chamber pot in the middle of his room served as his lavatory. He did not permit it to be moved. The pot had to remain in place until it could hold no more. And one day he even demanded from his landlord(?) a much more voluminous pot, so that it would need emptying less often.

There is something even better: here's what Madame Berger, née Martin, a former servant of Marcel Monnier, tells us: "Two or three times Monsieur Marcel Monnier went up to his room after lunch, to move his bowels in his chamber pot or his slop pail, and then brought it to me in the kitchen, where I was in the middle of lunch, for me to go empty it.

"On certain days he had his wife's bed removed from their shared bedroom to have it placed in the lavatory next door; then, having relieved himself in his chamber pot, he placed the pot on the night table next to his wife's bed, 'so that she smelled the odor well,' he would say. To be surer, he had closed the window.

"Monsieur Marcel Monnier had weak eyesight, even with his pince-nez. When he came into the kitchen, he leaned over the dishes, to the point of burning himself. It's true that he had a very poorly developed sense of smell. He didn't want the maids to go into his room, so that sometimes as a result, the pot into which he relieved himself was not emptied for several days, and he lived with a stink that seemed not to bother him."

There's no point in transcribing the five or six other depositions that only confirm this one.

All this explains how Monsieur Marcel Monnier could come each day to read the newspaper in his sister's room, as several witnesses inform us, without being disturbed by the excremental odor but on the contrary finding in it a sort of olfactory satisfaction. Nor, therefore, are we astonished that Marcel Monnier was not more indignant about circumstances that he himself would have willingly tolerated. These circumstances had come about little by little, through a gradual inurement. But other letters from Marcel Monnier, if we go far back, show us that at first he made some affectionate attempts to bring his sister back to a more normal way of life. On February 29, 1876, he wrote from Mont-de-Marsan: "My little

Gertrude,[13] today we are surrounded by masks and disguises. There is a big party at the town hall tonight. All the festivities are encouraged by splendid weather. I hope it's the same in Poitiers, *so that you can leave your cell,* and make a short trip to Blossac."[14] And on August 5, 1882, as a postcript to a letter written to his mother from Saint-Jean-de-Luz: "My little Gertrude, I cannot write to Booneen without sending you a little message, so that you see I haven't forgotten you. I hope you're not sick right now; take care of yourself; *wear a dress like everybody else,* and when I come back to Poitiers, which will be soon, we will go for a stroll together, if you'd like. It would be better, in any case, than to stay forever shut up in your room." Again, we read at the end of a letter to his mother from August 16, 1883: "Kiss Gertrude for me, and tell her that I haven't forgotten her, and that I'll write to her next time. Tell her to take care of herself and make up her mind to get some fresh air like everyone else."

These sentences, as Monsieur Barbier points out, show both a brother's solicitude and the totally voluntary nature of Mademoiselle Blanche Monnier's confinement.

Chapter 7

"The tendency to and habit of seclusion, which soon became total," said Monsieur Barbier in his lengthy report, "therefore existed in Mademoiselle Blanche Monnier as early as 1873, before her physical and moral powers were seriously weakened, when her father and grandfather were present to protect her and try to reason with her."

At the time Blanche Monnier was twenty-three years old. Different witnesses tell us that at this point, she was still "very gentle and good-natured." Yet her first mental problems seemed to have started appearing in 1871. Let's hear Monsieur Théodore Touchard, a plastering contractor:

"As a neighbor of the Demarconnay and Monnier families, I saw a lot of the Monnier children and their parents; the young girl, Made-

13. A name that he called his sister in private. Mademoiselle Blanche called her brother "Little Marcel." Both of them called their mother, Madame Monnier, "Booneen."
14. Tr. note: Blossac, a large municipal park in Poitiers dating from the eighteenth century, consists of more than 22 acres of walks overlooking the Clain Valley and includes an English garden.

moiselle Blanche Monnier, often came to the house when a small child; she was very lively and muddleheaded, a real pepperpot; we continued to see each other as neighbors for many years.

"At a certain time that I no longer recall, but that must have been when Mademoiselle Blanche was around twenty or twenty-two years old, my attention, and that of the neighbors, was drawn to the maneuvers of the young lady, who would go out with Madame Fazy, her maid, to a cul-de-sac where the son of Monsieur C—— lived; some time later there was a rumor that Mademoiselle Monnier would be marrying Monsieur C——, which surprised me and the neighbors, because of the age difference between them. Several months then went by without any marriage, and after that Mademoiselle Monnier stopped leaving her home and being seen; I heard tell that Madame Monnier hadn't wanted her daughter to marry Monsieur C—— because she thought he was too old. I repeat: starting from that moment, I never saw Mademoiselle Blanche again, and I know absolutely nothing about the decision that the Monnier family made about her."

The information available about Mademoiselle Blanche's condition before 1880 is very scarce. Marie Fazy, who worked for a long time as a servant for Madame Monnier, told us that at first, Mademoiselle Monnier wanted to be married; later she wanted to take her vows, and her mother was stubbornly against that. "The vexations experienced by Mademoiselle Monnier," said Marie Fazy, "caused a mental disturbance, but she was still able to think quite well about many subjects." But the time frame is not mentioned. There is likewise no date to situate the following statement by a certain Madame Honoré, née David, although it must precede the death of the elder Monsieur Monnier, which means before April 9, 1882:

"Sometimes Mademoiselle Blanche came down to the dining room to sing and play the piano; her mother would immediately push her back to her room, reprimanding her sharply and saying that "she was a disgrace." The sitting-room doors were closed to her. So Mademoiselle Blanche would go back up to her room, cursing, and right away Madame Monnier would send her husband to her daughter, to order her to be quiet."

It seems that, unfortunately, Madame Monnier's authoritarian personality grievously augmented her daughter's mental imbalance. Father Montbron, who knew the Monnier family for thirty-one years, describes Madame Monnier at that time as already "whimsical, severe, and imperious, as well as a tyrant." His contact with the family ceased abruptly, and when Father Montbron, who was surprised at not seeing Madame Monnier or her daughter any more, asked whether they had changed parishes or were ill, he was told that the two ladies no longer went out, not even to church. In 1882, when Father Montbron was called to give last rites to the elder Monsieur Monnier, who was dying, he learned from him the measures that he was obliged to take for his daughter, Blanche. "He possessed all his faculties," stated Father Montbron, and received the sacraments with full consciousness. He wept bitterly, seeming to show regret, either for having to give in to his wife's imperious demands by acting so strictly or for being forced to ward off scandal, for he said—and everyone already knew it by hearsay—that the young girl, a hysteric, undressed completely in front of everyone and displayed herself this way at the windows that looked out on to the street, which would explain, I suppose, the strict closing of these windows."

"She didn't want to put clothes on," declared Marie Deshoulières, née Brunet, who worked for Monsieur Demarconnay in 1883. "She went around the house wearing only a nightdress and bodice. . . . At this time, she wasn't mad; she reasoned excellently. She wasn't ill-tempered, except with her mother, whom she did not seem to love. When she talked with her, Mademoiselle Blanche often went into violent rages and might have turned to acts of brutality, had not Marie Fazy intervened. With her, and myself, she was gentle.

"Marie Fazy told me that Madame Monnier had always thwarted her daughter and always wanted to prevent her, even during her husband's lifetime, from going out; she always found a pretext for keeping the father from taking a walk with his daughter, and as she never went out, she didn't want Mademoiselle Blanche to go out on walks either."

At that time (1882) it seems that Blanche Monnier still came down to the dining room, where, Madame Deshoulières said, "she chatted with her mother very reasonably." Once she was back in her room, however, she was seized by terrors and "created ghosts out of everything. Believing that she saw men who were coming to get her, she would shout out, 'Help! Murder!' which could be heard in the street below."

"If you had come earlier," said Madame Blanchard, "in April 1882, you would have heard Mademoiselle Monnier yelling loudly, 'So justice no longer exists. I'm going to have you all put in prison, yes, all of you.' And this doubtless explains the weather stripping placed on the windows. They had not always been sealed, just the shutters, kept closed by a padlocked iron bar—clearly to prevent Mademoiselle Blanche from exposing herself. But she made up for it with her screaming. Then her mother told her that if she continued to scream in that way, a police superintendent would come to arrest her. When threats did not suffice, a broom was stuck out the window to push against the doorbell pull, to make her believe that it was the superintendent ringing." But she uncovered the ruse, and that's apparently when they began the custom of keeping the windows shut, even in summertime.

"For some time," we learn from Virginie Magault, née Neveux, "Mademoiselle Blanche asked every day for a paper and pencil in order to write. Her mother had them brought to her. She would write a letter that she placed in an envelope and addressed to different people whose names I no longer recall; then she slipped it between the blinds of her window, so that it fell into the courtyard, and told Marie Fazy, the cook, to have it taken to the post office. I was often chosen to do as Madame Monnier told me, to go out by the service door and come back in through the main door, so that the girl really believed that I was taking the letter to the post office. Once I got back, I would give it to Madame Monnier, who told me that when she threw others down, they shouldn't be opened, because they contained nothing important.

"The young lady did not want to see her mother, whom she called Boodeen, or Booneen, and in a single week, when she came to see her, she threw six chamberpots at her that broke on the stairway. Then Madame Monnier told her that she wouldn't give her any others, and she would leave her in her filth, to which her daughter replied that she was already in it; she even told her often that she wasn't the favorite one in the house."

Reading the testimony and the reports allows us to judge Monsieur Monnier's behavior less harshly; his sister's confinement seems to us partly justified, and moreover, we see that it was less a question of confinement than seclusion, to a great extent voluntary, despite screams, calls for help, and the remarkable inconsistencies of an unbalanced personality. What's more, the Barbier report established that Madame Monnier was "not even guilty of having imposed her ideas about that."

"Monsieur and Madame Monnier seem to have believed, like almost all people from their generation, in now-outdated notions.

"It was the elder Monsieur Monnier who decided that his daughter would be cared for at home by her parents, because it had been done so for six or seven years during his lifetime.

"He even expressed his decision with a certain paternal eloquence when he said in 1878 to Mademoiselle Kaenka: 'So long as I can care for her with doctors, I will keep her.'

"Faithful to her husband's intention, Madame Monnier showed that she was as attached to it as he had been when she replied to Mademoiselle Perroche, who spoke with her about putting her daughter in a nursing home "that she had vowed to stay with her daughter until her death."

Mademoiselle Blanche Monnier's easy improvement after she entered the hospital made some people hope for the full recovery of her reason. The doctors remained skeptical: "From a mental point of view," they said, "we consider Mademoiselle Blanche Monnier as a defective, whose reasoning is much poorer than normal."

On several occasions the examining magistrate tried to question her. He never found her in a condition allowing her to be sworn in. The results of the last try, on August 6, after two-and-a-half months of skilled hospital care that should have improved Mademoiselle Monnier's mental condition, were this possible, were as unfortunate as the previous ones. Moreover, three pathologists who were consulted expressed certainty that Mademoiselle Monnier would never regain her reason. Here is the transcript of the August 6 hearing:

Q: "Tell us your first and last names."

Mademoiselle Monnier begins to laugh, saying: "Nothing at all, nothing at all."

Q: "Isn't your name Blanche Monnier?"

A: "There isn't only one woman with that name."

Q: "How old are you?"

A: "I don't want to tell all that."

Q: "Where were you born?"

Mademoiselle Blanche Monnier utters some unintelligible words. However, we can make out this phrase: "But one can't stay here forever."

Q: "Don't you have a brother?"

A: "Well, then! Yes."

Q: "Will you tell us the name of your brother?"

Mademoiselle Monnier breaks out laughing and doesn't reply.

Q: "You do not want to tell us his name?"

A: "No."

Q: "Isn't your brother married?"

She replies in an unintelligible manner.

Q: "Didn't you go to your brother's wedding at Mont-de-Marsan?"

A: "Well, then, yes!"

Q: "Don't you have a niece, and can you tell us her name?"

A: "Too bad for her."

Q: "When you were a young girl, didn't Mademoiselle Gilbert give you piano lessons?"

A: "I don't know her."

Q: "In what boarding school were you brought up?"

A: "F——. One can't say everything."

Q: "Didn't your father take care of you and teach you Greek?"

A: "No."

Q: "Didn't you have Marie Fazy as your maid for a long time?"

A: "Yes."

Q: "What has become of that maid? Isn't she dead?"

A: "I don't know."

Q: "Where do you live in Poitiers?"

A: "And I don't want to say nothing at all. It's not for me to talk."

Q: "Didn't you live at 21 rue de la Visitation?"

A: "Yes, but it isn't 21, it's 14."

Q: "Wasn't there a nice yard there?"

A: "Yes, yes, when I get back there, I'll jump on the spine of another one."

Q: "What floor did you live on?"

Mademoiselle Monnier seems angry and speaks words that we are unable to grasp.

Q: "Was your room prettier than this one?"

A: "When we were at dear-good-great-Back, *it was better than here,* but we have to wait some more before going there."

Q: "Do you remember your father? Did you like him?"

A: "Oh! yes."

Q: "Is your father dead?"

Mademoiselle Monnier starts to laugh and tells us: "I don't know all that."

Q: "Do you remember your mother? Did she love you and did you love her?"

At this moment Mademoiselle Monnier becomes angry and says that she doesn't want to talk.

Q: "Would you like to see your mother?"

A: "No, it's better for her to stay where she is."

Q: "So then you don't love your mother?"

A: "Yes, yes, but it's better for her to stay where she is."

Q: "Haven't you been told that your mother is dead?"

Mademoiselle Monnier starts to laugh and does not reply. After a few moments, she says: "She is still at dear-good-great-Back."

Q: "Did your brother come to see you often when you lived on the rue de la Visitation?"

A: "Yes, yes."

Q: "Did he bring you sweets?"

A: "We are quite rich enough at dear-good-great-Back to buy pastries." (Hearing us dictate this reply, Mademoiselle Monnier bursts out laughing.)

Q: "On the rue de la Visitation, did you sleep in a very clean bed, and did you have very white sheets?"

A: "What would one say at dear-good-great-Back if one heard all that."

Q: "Why did you keep a veil or blanket over your face?"

Mademoiselle Monnier throws out a string of words that we cannot grasp.

Q: "Did they wash you and comb your hair when you lived on the rue de la Visitation?"

A: "It wasn't me who had so much hair; that was another one. There are others apart from myself who have the same name."

(Many other equally irrational replies follow.)

Chapter 8

Almost all the information that we have given about this strange case would be developed only in the previously mentioned report by Barbier, Marcel Monnier's lawyer, which he presented to the prosecuting chamber as part of his client's opposition to the examining magistrate's ruling that sent Monsieur Monnier to be tried by competent authority for criminal confinement and torture, a capital crime under article 344 of the penal code. We are surprised not that Marcel Monnier was acquitted on appeal after having been sentenced by the criminal court but rather that the prosecuting chamber that sent him to criminal court on October 7, 1901, could have acknowledged—it is not known how—

(1) that, if there was no cause to prosecute Monsieur Monnier for arbitrary confinement, by contrast, there was "against the said Monsieur Monnier sufficient evidence that he did willfully . . . carry out on the person of his sister, Blanche, violences of the nature of those provided for and punished by article 311 of the penal code.

"Or, at least, of having been a party to the said crime of violence specified above, by aiding and abetting the perpetrator of said violence(?) with knowledge of the acts that were committed; crime provided for and punished by articles 58 and 60 of the penal code."

Nothing in the least was proven, as we have seen. Therefore we feel there is no point in presenting the highly insufficient arguments and speeches from the criminal court.

Here is the appellate court's decree:

"After having deliberated in accordance with the law:

"Whereas it emerges from the preliminary investigation and proceedings that the internment or confinement of Mademoiselle Monnier was necessitated by her mental condition;

"and that for the first years of her confinement, she was given the necessary care, but that after her father's death and although some documents and above all the will of the widow Monnier show that she felt affection for her daughter, however intermittent and irregular, Blanche Monnier had been left for many years in a room without air or light, on a filthy pallet and an indescribable state of squalor;

"and that although she was not deprived of abundant and even costly food, the total lack of supervision and care rendered this precaution useless, and without the court's opportune intervention, the barbarous methods that governed her treatment would soon have had a fatal outcome for her;

"whereas these deeds have rightly evoked public reproach, and place upon the widow Monnier's posthumous memory a moral responsibility whose gravity cannot be exaggerated;

"but whereas in what regards more specifically Marcel Monnier, the facts of the case do not fall under the power of a penal provision;

"and that indeed, a crime of violence or assault and battery cannot be asserted where there is no violence—and no such act has been proven against Monnier or his mother, apart from the act of confinement, for which the prosecution chamber has determined to fall outside the legal definition of violence, and if some jurists believe that a crime of omission may sometimes take its place, this does not signify that this omission imposes a legally incumbent duty on its perpetrator;

"whereas it is true that the law of April 19, 1898, punished the act of anyone who deprives a minor under the age of fifteen of necessary food or care to the point of compromising his health, but this new law has not been extended to apply to the insane;

"and that it presumes inherently that the minor thus being deprived of care has been entrusted to, at least in the matter of that care, the person who is denying it;

"whereas it does not appear that Monnier was ever in this situation with respect to his sister;

"that in the last weeks of her life no more than before did the widow

Monnier permit any undermining of her absolute authority, above all from a son who did not live with her, whom she did not love, and whom she had disinherited;

"and that the mission she had conferred on him during this last period, that of watching over his sister, in no way implied any abandonment of her authority;

"and that in any event, it is not proven that she did so, which Monnier always denied, and the categorical testimony as well as deeds by servants who would have been charged with carrying it out clearly exclude it;

"and that in any case it is in no way proven that the appealing party participated with a conscious and premeditated will either as coperpetrator or accessory, or should be considered as legally criminal and punishable for the deeds of which his mother appears to have been the only one responsible;

"and that doubtless, despite his infirmities, only partial, furthermore, it is impossible to believe that Monnier was ignorant of the deplorable condition in which his sister was left and that the purely passive role to which he felt obliged to limit himself, as well as the cold impassivity that allowed him to make no useful intervention, deserves the harshest reprimand;

"and that nevertheless, his conduct not falling under the power of the penal law, to which the judges may make no addition, there are grounds for the court to declare his acquittal.

"ON THESE GROUNDS:

"In place of the sentence read on October 11, 1901, by the criminal court of Poitiers,

"it is decided that it was wrongly adjudicated, and successfully appealed;

"consequently, said sentence is reversed;

"amending and doing what the first judges should have done and without there taking place any other accession to evidential conclusions:

"Monnier is to be discharged without costs.

"so tried and decided in open session of the court of appeals, criminal chamber, at Poitiers, on November 20, 1901."

ANDRE GIDE (1869–1951), an acknowledged giant of twentieth-century literature, has been honored not only for his fiction, criticism, and editorial work for periodicals and books publishers but also for his extraordinary journals. He was awarded the Nobel Prize for literature in 1947.

BENJAMIN IVRY is the author of *Francis Poulenc* (1996), *Arthur Rimbaud* (1998), and *Maurice Ravel: A Life* (2000), as well as *Paradise for the Portuguese Queen,* a poetry collection. He has also translated Olivier Todd's *Albert Camus* (1997) and Jules Verne's *Magellania* (2000), as well as Adam Zagajewski's *Canvas* (1992), the last in collaboration with Renata Gorczynski.

The University of Illinois Press
is a founding member of the
Association of American University Presses.

Composed in 10.5/13 Adobe Minion
by Barbara Evans
at the University of Illinois Press
Manufactured by Thomson-Shore, Inc.

University of Illinois Press
1325 South Oak Street
Champaign, IL 61820-6903
www.press.uillinois.edu